# Guarantee You Are Understood
## and *Not Just Heard*

### Part of the
### Guarantee You Are Understood Initiative

### Phyllis Cronbaugh

Copyright ©2018 by Phyllis Cronbaugh

All rights reserved. Copying or reproducing portions of this book is strictly prohibited (except where expressly noted in Appendix H – Book Club Questions for Discussion and Appendix I – Book Club Answers); this includes storing in a retrieval system or transmitting in any form or by any means – electronic, mechanical, photocopying, recording, or otherwise – without express written permission of the publisher. No patent liability is assumed concerning the use of the information contained herein. The publisher and the author assume no responsibility for errors or omissions. Neither is any liability assumed for damages resulting from the use of the information contained herein.

Artwork Property of Phyllis Cronbaugh
Provided by Fotolia.com

ISBN: 9781730951893
ASIN: 1730951899
Published by: Phyllis Cronbaugh
Life Transition Solutions LLC
1716 E Cedar St #3, Olathe, KS, 66062 USA

https://www.GuaranteeYouAreUnderstood.com/
Facebook: Guarantee You Are Understood Initiative
pcronbaugh@gmail.com
1-816-820-5196

Printed in the United States of America
Published March 2010 (First Version – Published as *The Talking Stick: Guarantee You Are Understood and Not Just Heard*
Published by Dancing on the Edge, LLC

Printed in Seoul, Korea
Published December 2014 (Korean Version – Book Herb Publishing
Translation rights arranged through Enters Korea Co, Ltd, Seoul, Korea

# Acknowledgments

Blessings and gratitude to all the teachers and elders who so willingly shared their knowledge over the years. I now teach what you shared so this wisdom will be carried forward to the next seven generations.

I thank Michael Kravets of MTK Consulting, LLC for his editing skills and the creative ideas he shared. I highly recommend Michael to help with your next writing project. See Appendix E – Resources.

Teresa and Lori of Point Graphics, I love our MisUnderstood Grannies and thank you for your graphic design work on the book covers. See Appendix E – Resources and Chapter 8 – Stories and Examples for the Grannies.

Jim Grant of Simply Creative Media. Great job on the new Guarantee You Are Understood Initiative website. See Appendix E – Resources and https://GuaranteeYouAreUnderstood.com.

I thank the individuals, clients, and students whose stories I have used in this book and my classes over the years. I have learned as much from you as you learned from me.

Love to Cindy B for her inspiration of how the *Guarantee You Are Understood Initiative* could benefit the countless organizations who fight vigilantly to be understood. And, untold gratitude to those who took the time to read the first draft of this book and give feedback. It takes a village to raise a child... and turn a manuscript into a book. I appreciate Laura and Shari for their cooperation in one of the photos. Thanks, Kari, for letting me photograph your talking stick and to Tom for the amazing grapevine stick. Ben and TJ, you did a great job on your yarn talking sticks and it is my pleasure to include a picture in this book. I know I've missed someone. Know that I sincerely appreciate your help.

And, finally, I recognize my mother, Beverley Murphy, who instilled in me at an early age the desire to write down my thoughts.

# Dedication

I dedicate this book to all those individuals with whom I have had differences in the past. May we meet again and resolve the conflict.

# Testimonials

"I don't know how we would have gotten through my son's teen years without our talking stick. I feel confident today that our sessions are what kept him off drugs and got him through school. And, I'm proud to say that he continues to use the stick in his family circle today." Kelly – Scottsdale, AZ

"To say we were at the end of the rope with Rachel is an understatement. Her illness consumed our whole family. Once she began talking and admitted her circumstances, there was a shift like turning on a light. Today, we're able to help, and all our futures are much brighter. I don't believe it would have happened without our Talking Stick sessions. Blessings to you." Rachel's Mom – KC, MO

"When I heard of #MeToo movement, I knew I had to finally talk to my husband of ten years about experiences I'd had growing up. I'd never told a soul and probably wouldn't have if I hadn't been able to hold a talking stick. We both have better understandings of each other. Thanks." Tracy – OP, KS

"I can't say that the Talking Stick saved my marriage, but it made the separation amicable. Today, my ex-wife and I are friends, and I didn't think that would ever happen." John – Los Angeles, CA

"I don't have stats on success and failure in the direct marketing business model, but I was ready to give up. Who would have thought a silly Wheel of Fortune game would give me the impetus to get to where I am today? Amazing. And, it just keeps on growing." Mike – St. Louis, MO

"When I suggested using a talking stick at a corporate function, I thought I would get laughed out of the room, but I didn't. When the project was complete it had gone so well, I got a letter of commendation from the president of the company." David – Wrightwood, CA

A young boy told me in confidence that his parents needed to know about the bullying he received at school, but he was reluctant to say anything. He said his father was big on *we don't air our dirty laundry in public*. I couldn't see how being bullied was dirty laundry, but somehow the boy did. He wanted to know if using a talking stick would make it easier to talk to his dad. I told him he needed to decide. Once he held the stick, he closed his eyes, and a huge smile slowly spread across his face. "Yeah," he said, "It works." Tyler (9 years old) – North Kansas City, MO

# Table of Contents

Acknowledgments ..................................................................... 5
Dedication ................................................................................. 7
Testimonials ............................................................................. 7
Table of Contents .................................................................... 9
What is the Guarantee You Are Understood Initiative? ....... 19
Prologue ................................................................................. 21
   Book Clubs ........................................................................ 22
How to Get the Most Out of this Book ................................. 23
Chapter 1 ................................................................................ 25
What Is a Talking Stick? Where Did They Originate? ........... 25
   Talking Stick Sessions ...................................................... 25
   Talking Sticks, the Tools .................................................. 25
   Neanderthal Rituals in France ......................................... 26
   The Ancient Greeks .......................................................... 26
   Illustrations in Ancient Art .............................................. 27
   The Iroquois Confederacy and Our Founding Fathers .... 28
   We the People of the United States................................ 29
   Baton, Wand, Staff, Scepter or Stick? ............................. 29
Chapter 2 ................................................................................ 31
The Guarantee and the 10 Rules of Engagement ................ 31
      It's Everyone's Right ................................................... 32
      The Negative Spiral .................................................... 32
      Natural Tendencies .................................................... 32
      Disconnected and Isolated ......................................... 33
   The Guarantee .................................................................. 33
   The 10 Rules of Engagement ........................................... 34
Chapter 3 Dad and the "D" Grade .......................................... 43

Actual Personal/Family Talking Stick Example ........................... 43
Chapter 4 .................................................................................... 48
Splitting the Group ..................................................................... 48
Actual Organization/Business Talking Stick Example with Multiple Segments .................................................................................... 48
    The History ............................................................................ 48
    The Talking Stick Session ....................................................... 53
    Win-Win or Lose-Lose ............................................................ 54
    Welcoming Session ................................................................ 56
    Fact Finding Session .............................................................. 58
  Conflict Resolution Session ..................................................... 68
    Difficult Discussion Session ................................................... 73
Chapter 5 .................................................................................... 77
Types of Talking Sticks ................................................................ 77
  What Type of Talking Stick Do You Need? .............................. 77
  Personal-Family Talking Sticks ................................................ 78
  Start at An Early Age ............................................................... 80
  Welcoming Sessions ............................................................... 81
    Get Creative ........................................................................... 81
    Guidance for Participants ...................................................... 81
  Brainstorming and Fact Finding Sessions ............................... 82
    The Difference Between Brainstorming and Fact Finding .... 82
  Difficult Discussions ................................................................ 84
    Courage Found ...................................................................... 84
    Agreeing to Disagree ............................................................. 84
    Intending to Disagree ............................................................ 85
  Conflict Resolution .................................................................. 85
    Lawsuit or Litigation vs. Mediation ....................................... 85
    Facilitators Should Be Mandatory ......................................... 86

Chapter 6 ................................................................................. 87
Planning Your Session ........................................................... 87
   Is a Talking Stick Session Appropriate for Your Topic or Group? ..... 87
   Who's Who in a Talking Stick? ............................................. 89
      Designated Listener ........................................................ 89
   Purpose, Desired Result, Barometer Indicator, Completion Status. 90
      The Purpose ................................................................... 90
      Determine the Desired Result ......................................... 91
      Use a Barometer Indicator to Gauge Progress ................. 92
      Not Knowing When to Shut Up ....................................... 93
      Completion Status .......................................................... 94
   Merging Types of Talking Sticks ........................................... 94
   NO Punishment NO Discipline .............................................. 95
   Leaders and Facilitators ....................................................... 96
      Definition of a Leader ..................................................... 96
      Definition of a Facilitator ................................................ 96
      Additional Leader and Facilitator Duties ......................... 96
      Certified Guarantee You Are Understood Initiative Facilitators and Coaches ......................................................................... 97
   Determine the Location for a Session .................................. 97
   Formats and Styles Opening, Rotation, Closing .................. 98
      Personal or Family Format .............................................. 98
      Personal/Family Format with a Facilitator ...................... 99
      Wheel Format with Circle Style with a Leader ................ 99
      Wheel Format with Circle Style with a Facilitator ......... 100
      Wheel Format with Popcorn Style with Leader or Facilitator .... 100
      Theater Format with a Leader or Facilitator ................. 101
      Q&A Combo ................................................................... 102
   The Guarantee and Proper Passing Protocol ..................... 103

- The Speaker is Finished ............................................................. 103
- The Designated Listener ............................................................ 104
- Deal Breaker – Deal Maker ........................................................ 104
- The Simplest Form ...................................................................... 104
- The Extra Mile ............................................................................. 105
- The Speaker is Complete ........................................................... 105
- Proper Passing Protocol ............................................................. 105
- The Gift of Respect ..................................................................... 106
- Differences in Formats ............................................................... 106
- Frame of Reference .................................................................... 107
- Omitting the Guarantee ............................................................. 107

Passing on Your Right to Speak ....................................................... 108
Plan Your Opening ............................................................................ 109
Begin in a Positive Space ................................................................. 110
Establishing a Collective .................................................................. 111
Timer and Recorder .......................................................................... 112
Multiple Points of Discussion and Notetaking ............................. 113
Removing Someone from a Session .............................................. 113
Ending a Session When the Barometer Indicates ....................... 114
- Completion Status ....................................................................... 114
- The Desired Result is Achieved – Successful ........................... 114
- The Desired Result is Not Reached – Stalemate or Agreeing to Disagree ............................................................................. 116

Closing ................................................................................................ 117
Get Agreement .................................................................................. 118
Open, Truthful, Heart-to-Heart Communication ......................... 118

Chapter 7 ............................................................................................ 119
Speaker and Listener Tips and Etiquette ...................................... 119
- Speaker Tips and Etiquette ....................................................... 119

- Ground Before Beginning ............................................................ 119
- Make an Eye Connection ............................................................ 119
- Criticism ........................................................................................ 120
- Show Confidence – Read It If You Need To ............................. 120
- Trauma – Drama with the Designated Listener ...................... 120
- The Speaker's Best Response – I Guess I Didn't Make Myself Clear ................................................................................................... 121
- Never Try to Change Another's View Through Manipulation .... 122
- When the Speaker is Finished ................................................. 122
- Passing the Talking Stick ......................................................... 122

Designated Listener Tips and Etiquette ........................................ 123
- The Designated Listener Accomplishes the Guarantee ........... 123
- Always Start With… ................................................................. 123
- Stay in the Present .................................................................. 124
- Be an Adult .............................................................................. 124
- Keep an Open Mind ................................................................. 125
- Walk in the Speaker's Shoes ................................................... 126
- Promoting Respect and Boosting Self-esteem ........................ 126
- Trauma – Drama Repeating Keywords, But Not Mimicking ..... 127
- Trauma – Drama Queen .......................................................... 128
- The Speaker Tries to Sway Your Opinion ................................ 129
- Take Notes if Allowed ............................................................. 129

Chapter 8 ......................................................................................... 131
Stories and Examples ..................................................................... 131
- Guarantee You Are Understood Lighter Side ......................... 131
- Personal/Family Sessions ........................................................ 131
  - The Youngest Talking Stick Facilitator ................................ 131
  - Best Friends Nancy and Sue ................................................ 132

- Nancy's Opening at the Park .................................................... 134
- Welcoming Sessions ................................................................. 134
  - A Sisterhood Welcoming Session ........................................ 134
  - Break the Ice or Get Down to Business? ............................. 135
  - Who Moved the Chocolate? ................................................ 136
- Brainstorming Sessions ............................................................ 136
  - Brainstorming for the Holidays .......................................... 136
  - Wheel of Fortune FABs ........................................................ 137
- Fact Finding Sessions ............................................................... 140
  - The Home-court Advantage ................................................ 140
  - Just Getting the Facts .......................................................... 141
- Difficult Discussions ................................................................. 143
  - Two Sets of Rules ................................................................. 143
  - Amy's Eating Disorder ......................................................... 143
  - Nicos and Erin ...................................................................... 144
  - The Italian Mother-in-Law .................................................. 145
- Conflict Resolution Sessions ................................................... 145
  - Joyce and Don's Child Custody Session .............................. 145
  - Joyce's Opening for the Child Custody Session ................. 146
  - Town Council Mediation in Colorado ................................. 147
  - Town Council Mediation Introduction .............................. 148
  - The Trade Show Conflict ..................................................... 148
  - The Fifteen-step Action Plan .............................................. 150
  - Mutiny in Arizona ................................................................ 151
- Other Stories ............................................................................ 153
  - The Fidgety Young Woman ................................................. 153
  - The Story of Maynard and Steve ......................................... 155
  - Revealing Ulterior Motives .................................................. 155

| | |
|---|---|
| There's Never Only One Way to Do Anything | 157 |
| Walking Around the Wheel | 157 |

## Appendix A ......................................................................... 159
## Make Your Own Talking Stick ............................................ 159

| | |
|---|---|
| Native American Traditions | 159 |
| Use Your Imagination | 160 |
| Making Your Talking Stick using Native Traditions | 162 |
| Use Your Tradition | 167 |
| Lastly, and Most Important | 167 |

## Appendix B ......................................................................... 169
## Guarantee You are Understood Initiative ........................ 169

| | |
|---|---|
| What is the Initiative? | 169 |
| Books | 169 |
| Wild Woman Rites of Empowerment Bible - Over 50 Life-Changing Ceremonies | 169 |
| Tyler's First Talking Stick (Children's Book) and *Parents, Help Your Child Find Their Voice* (two books in one) | 170 |
| Erase Your Past – Change the Future | 170 |
| Guarantee You Are Understood Facilitator's Certification Guidebook (available 2019 – preorder today). | 170 |
| Guarantee You Are Understood Coach's Certification Guidebook (available 2019 – preorder today) | 171 |

## Appendix C ......................................................................... 173
## About Phyllis Cronbaugh .................................................. 173

| | |
|---|---|
| Native American and Indigenous Training | 173 |
| National Speakers' Association and Writing | 173 |
| Real Estate | 174 |
| Family | 174 |
| Past Training and Speaking Corporate Clients | 175 |

- Appendix D .................................................................................... 177
- Other Books by Phyllis Cronbaugh ................................................... 177
  - These Books are Available on Amazon.com ................................ 177
  - Business ........................................................................................ 177
    - Selling with NO Selling Business Strategies ............................ 177
  - Real Estate .................................................................................... 177
    - Strategic Short Sales: Morally Wrong or Financially Prudent? .. 177
  - Shamanic Fiction .......................................................................... 178
    - Saving the Crystal Skull: An Adventure of Mayan 2012 Prophecy ................................................................................................ 178
    - Discovering the Magickal Mysterious Character ..................... 178
  - Shamanic Non-fiction ................................................................... 179
    - The Talking Stick – Guarantee You Are Understood and Not Just Heard – Korean version (2014) ............................................... 179
- Appendix E ...................................................................................... 181
- Resources ........................................................................................ 181
  - Michael Kravets, MTK Consulting ............................................. 181
  - Point Graphics, Teresa Carnes and Lori Snow .......................... 181
- Appendix F ...................................................................................... 183
- Simple Talking Stick Structure ......................................................... 183
  - Opening a Talking Stick ............................................................. 183
  - Rules of Engagement .................................................................. 184
  - Talking Stick Dialog .................................................................... 186
  - Announcing the Completion Status and Ending the Session ..... 187
  - Closing a Session ........................................................................ 187
  - A Simple Welcoming Session ..................................................... 188
- Appendix G ..................................................................................... 189
- Questionnaire for ............................................................................ 189
- Utilizing Strengths of the Participants ............................................. 189

Appendix H ................................................................................ 191
Book Club Questions for Discussion .................................................. 191
Appendix I ................................................................................. 195
Book Club Answers ....................................................................... 195

# What is the Guarantee You Are Understood Initiative?

The Initiative's vision is advocacy for today's kids, teens, young adults, or anyone needing the courage to find their voice[1]. No one expresses our mission better than Whitney Houston in *Greatest Love of All*.

... "No matter what they take from me they can't take away my dignity. ... I found the greatest love of all inside of me. ... Learning to love yourself is the greatest love of all."

The Initiative's goal is three-fold.

- One. To provide a means for individuals to be 100% understood and not just heard during difficult conversations or conflict resolution. Our approach instills confidence and unique advantages to anyone needing to find their voice.

- Two. To help victims and survivors of abuse overcome emotional trauma and regain dignity. Our methods help individuals repair a broken spirit and retake their power.

- Three. Work with individuals to identify negative behavior patterns in their lives, take responsibility, assume authority, and stand accountable for every thought, word, and deed.

Every aspect of the Initiative promotes respect and boosts self-esteem. The results are balanced individuals who know their self-worth, demand recognition in society and are ready to take on the world.

---

[1] Causes include but are certainly not limited to: bullying, domestic abuse (emotional, physical, mental and sexual in children, spouses, and elders), substance abuse, eating disorders, unwanted pregnancy, teen suicide, peer pressure, prejudice (hate crimes, racial profiling), and many more.

Our unique methods fall outside the realm of techniques currently used in therapy but are not new; they were used in the earliest times to move and focus energy to intensify the healing process. They are not meant to replace techniques currently used in therapy but to complement and enhance your strategies and may, at times, be the breakthrough approach that gets results.

You don't need several sets of three-letter designations trailing after your name indicating counselor, masters, or doctoral degrees, to understand the process, although we welcome anyone who is dedicated to coaching, therapy, counseling, or mentoring. For those without the three-letter clusters, the alchemical structure of the ancient process supplements and enhances intuitive skills to help anyone assist others in healing themselves.

This book is just one of the tools in the Initiative. Check out the website https://www.GuaranteeYouAreUnderstood.com for more information.

You can make a difference.

# Prologue

The original publication of this book came out in 2010 under the title *The Talking Stick: Guarantee You Are Understood and Not Just Heard*. It's still available on Amazon.

Between 2012-2014 I worked with a Korean publishing company to translate the text into Korean. How this came about is amusing, and you can read the whole story on the website.

This all-new edition incorporates additional aspects and explores exciting new areas. There are a dozen more stories and numerous additional examples of successful Talking Stick sessions and unique ideas of how to tackle situations that require multiple functions within a single session. Diagrams clearly explain the different formats, styles, and rotation options. The entire planning section is expanded to give you a wealth of alternatives for using Talking Sticks within your organization to create effective, memorable functions.

When you are *understood and not just heard*, you feel something magical happen because it is so rare in our society today that someone actually listens, and of course as a speaker with a talking stick you are Guaranteed to be understood.

Grandmother Elsie, a Cherokee elder, once said:

> ...the mystery and magick of the talking stick are where truth occurs – the manifestation of true heart-to-heart communication.

Magick is not misspelled. Today we associate magic with *sleight of hand*, trickery, or illusion. The ancients didn't consider this aspect; their word *magick* indicated an alchemical change, or *change at the cellular level*, which native people believe happens when souls connect.

The spelling doesn't matter if we connect and truly understand each other's perspective. Enjoy this new version and discover the magick.

## Book Clubs

Appendix H contains numerous questions, and thought-provoking scenarios for use in book club discussions and Appendix I is my answers. You may have more ideas. I would love to hear back from you. Email me at pcronbaugh@gmail.com.

*Phyllis Cronbaugh*

# How to Get the Most Out of this Book

Organizing this book was tough. My editor, Michael[2], asked me if I expected my audience to read from start to finish or to jump around and use the book as a reference manual. I told him, both.

I've used numerous stories to make specific points, and sometimes a story fits in several places. I decided to put most of the illustrations together in Chapter 8 – Stories and Examples, but then Michael said a writer should never refer readers to a place further on in a book, only to previous text. That made sense but seemed impossible to comply with because of all the elements I was connecting. So, there are times when you will need to jump forward to see an example, and I hope this isn't confusing.

The second reason for pulling the stories and examples out of the beginning chapters is to streamline the planning process for experienced facilitators using the text for reference. They will most likely be familiar with the stories and their primary objective after they understand the process will be to plan for contingencies and create engaging, productive sessions.

Then there is Chapter 3 – Dad and the "D" Grade and Chapter 4 – Splitting the Group. You might consider them stories and wonder why they aren't with the rest of the examples. They are actual Talking Stick dialog and not stories, except for the background of the individuals. I felt these two actual examples should be toward the beginning for readers who are reading straight through from the beginning or are new to the process and know nothing about Talking Stick sessions. Dad and the "D" Grade is an example of the simplest type of Talking Stick session, except for a Welcoming process. Splitting the Group shows a complicated session generally used in business scenarios. The event I describe involved a women's sorority.

At one time I had the order of Chapter 5 – Types of Talking Sticks and Chapter 6 – Planning Your Session switched. Most newcomers to designing Talking Stick sessions feel they should know the *type* initially to plan effectively. But, many times it's like Steven Covey stresses in

---

[2] See Appendix E – Resources for information on Michael Kravets and MTK Consulting.

his well-known book, *The 7 Habits of Highly Effective People*, "Begin with the end in mind." Sometimes, as you will see, it makes more sense to determine the *purpose*, *desired result*, *barometer indicator*, or even the *completion status* first. After making those decisions, the type of session should be clear, if it wasn't before. Definitions and considerations for planning sessions are in Chapter 6.

Here's a summary of the organization:

- **History** – Chapter 1 – What is a Talking Stick? Where Did They Originate?
- **Foundation and principles of the process** – Chapter 2 – The Guarantee and the 10 Rules of Engagement
- **Dialog from a simple Talking Stick session** – Chapter 3 – Dad and the "D" Grade
- **Dialog from a complex Talking Stick session** – Chapter 4 – Splitting the Group
- **The 5 Types of Talking Stick sessions described in this book** – Chapter 5 – Types of Talking Sticks
- **Definitions and Considerations for planning a Talking Stick session** – Chapter 6 – Planning Your Talking Stick
- **Considerations and tips for participating individuals** – Chapter 7 – Speakers and Listeners Tips and Etiquette
- **Stories and examples that support each section** – Chapter 8 – Stories and Examples

For the diligent individual, the Facilitator's and Coach's Certification Guidebook will be available in 2019. See Appendix B – Guarantee You are Understood Initiative.

# Chapter 1
# What Is a Talking Stick?
# Where Did They Originate?

A *talking stick* is a simple communication tool that can be used by five-year-olds to one-hundred-five-year-olds. And, the techniques described here are just as effective in the kitchen as they are in the conference room.

## Talking Stick Sessions

Use a Talking Stick session to:

- help everyone feel welcome at a meeting,
- clarify and establish relationship agreements,
- settle a dispute, conflict, or argument,
- clear the air before disruptions occur,
- bring mutual benefit and welfare,
- bring order to unfinished business,
- brainstorm for creative insight,
- find a solution to a challenge,
- achieve a consensus within a group, or
- help structure a group into a cohesive team.

No matter what your need for better communication, a Talking Stick process is efficient and effective.

## Talking Sticks, the Tools

Talking sticks, the actual tools that are used, are as individual as the speakers and listeners who use them. A dead branch can be picked up in the woods. If a situation arises and you must have a stick immediately, a pen or pencil or some other object at hand can work fine. New age groups may pass a feather to honor the native people who brought the principals to North America originally. For many individuals, families, and groups their talking stick is a prized possession. Some are custom designed, hand carved and quite expensive, others embellished with organizational logos, and some personal sticks are shaped over time honoring a family lineage.

There is only one rule when making a talking stick; use your imagination and put your heart into the project. Appendix A – Make Your Own Talking Stick is devoted to this subject.

**The rest of this book will show you how to use your talking stick in a "Talking Stick session" and how to create and design your discussion or gathering.**

## *Neanderthal Rituals in France*

No one knows when the tradition of holding a stick gave someone *license to speak without interruption,* but the practice is ancient. Archeologists have found depictions in paintings and artifacts they termed *batons made of bone* in the Tue d'Audoubert cave in France. They are intricately carved and decorated and appear to have been used in rituals by Neanderthals. We don't know if they were talking sticks or merely symbols of power, but it is evident that whoever carried them held a position of respect in the community.

## *The Ancient Greeks*

In the *Anger of the Achilles* (Robert Graves translation of the *Iliad*), Achilles announces to the War Council that he is withdrawing from the battle of Troy and he takes a vow on the *gold studded wand, which gave him the right to uninterrupted speech*. The War with Troy occurred around 1200 BCE. Another mention of a wand comes in this Greek poem about Zeus:

> By this dry wand no more to sprout
> Or put green twigs or foliage out,
> Since once the hatchet, swinging free
> Cross-chopped it from a mountain tree,
> Then trimmed away both leaves and bark.

> By this same wood, which men will mark
> Ancient traditions marked by Zeus,
> Have set to honorable use
> In ruling their debates: I vow,
> That all you Greeks assemble now
> Before me – mark these words.

## *Illustrations in Ancient Art*

Above left, an Egyptian deity, Hathor, consort of Horus and Ra holds a scepter and an ankh. The scepter is an indicator of her status, and the ankh represents her ideals of love and life. Right, Indra is known by different names; Lord of Heaven in the Vedic texts of Hinduism, a guardian deity in Buddhism, and King of the Highest Heaven in Jainism. In this Cambodian temple, he is surrounded by Apsaras, young, beautiful maidens that have mastered the art of celestial dance.

Above left, Augustus, known as Caesar Augustus or Octavius, is the first emperor of the Roman Empire; Julius Caesar's adopted son and heir is shown repeatedly with his staff of power. Right, Catherine the Great, Empress of Russia and the countries longest-ruling female leader. She is known for continuing the work of her late husband, Peter the Great.

Above left, Julius Caesar, one of the most potent Roman politicians and military general. Numerous statues show him carrying his staff. Right, Elizabeth I, Queen of England and Ireland. Also known as the Virgin Queen and the last of the monarchs in the House of Tudor. She carries her scepter of power and a ball symbolizing the world.

## *The Iroquois Confederacy and Our Founding Fathers*

The founding fathers of our nation led by Benjamin Franklin and Thomas Paine interacted with the natives of the Iroquois Confederacy or the League of Five Nations, which included the Cayuga, Seneca, Onondaga, Oneida, and the Mohawk tribes. Chiefs Hiawatha and Deganwidah, leaders at the time, recounted stories of the League's founding around 1000 CE. While our nation was searching for direction, the five nations had been at peace for 700 years under their constitution, the Kaianerekowa or Great Law of Peace.

One of the two traditions used to keep the peace was Talking Stick ceremonies. The second was their Council or Elders, which is discussed more in Chapter 2 – The Guarantee and the 10 Rules of Engagement/Rule 4: All Participants Are Equal.

## *We the People of the United States...*

An interesting fact is that George Washington appointed John Rutledge of South Carolina as the chairman of the Committee of Detail for the United States Constitution. Rutledge and his committee considered many documents of European and Middle Eastern origin but discarded them in favor of the Iroquois form of government.

Our constitution was written and begins...

> We the People of the United States in order to form a more perfect Union...

These words were taken directly from the Kaianerekowa. What is tragic is that the Confederacy's two founding principles of Talking Stick ceremonies and the organization of their councils, which kept their people at peace for 700 years has been forgotten by our government in the last 200 years.

## *Baton, Wand, Staff, Scepter or Stick?*

Today, a Talking Stick *session* (hereafter referred to as a "Talking Stick," or "Talking Sticks") can be used to help strangers feel like they've known each other for years or level playing fields between executives and workers. It can show how an issue has been taken entirely out of context and allow both sides to save face in a touchy situation.

Talking Sticks foster consideration and appreciation of differences instead of prejudging and labeling. After a Talking Stick, parties may still disagree, but because of the unique alchemy of the process, they generally see the other's opinion as valid and as a product of their frame of reference. Both sides may be more willing to compromise allowing a course of right action for the greater good.

# Chapter 2
# The Guarantee
# and the 10 Rules of Engagement

Think back on the most difficult conversation you've had in your life. Why was it so challenging? Would it have been easier if you'd known initially that you wouldn't be interrupted, judged or criticized, that your opinion would carry respect and be held in confidence if that was your wish? And, of course, there would have been a 100% Guarantee that you'd be understood. A Talking Stick session offers all this and more. Difficult conversations just got easier.

The Guarantee plus the Rules of Engagement form the backbone of Talking Stick sessions. Once you understand the reasoning behind the rules, you will be able to create additional processes.

I Googled *listening skills* and found several websites that professed to have ways to improve my ability to listen. I found an article called *10 Tips to Help You Develop Effective Listening Skills*. Another was *The Big 6: An Active Listening Skill Set*. All great information.

What I noticed though was that none of the sites included a **guarantee** that if I mastered their skills, I would understand precisely what the speaker intended. Or to take it one step further, if I was the speaker there was no **guarantee** that I would feel understood.

Now, to me, that was odd, because I believe in "guarantees." If someone goes by the Rules of Engagement and follows the steps in this book, the speaker is guaranteed to be understood.

### It's Everyone's Right

The Bill of Rights, the First Amendment to the Constitution of the United States, gives everyone the *right to free speech* among other freedoms. I take it one step further. I believe everyone deserves the right to not only free speech but to be understood.

### The Negative Spiral

Daily we damage relationships because of poor or lack of communication. We base decisions on what we *think* we hear or *believe* someone meant. In Western society especially, we spend too much time in our heads analyzing situations, and our egos refuse to rest until they have determined the reason for something to have occurred. Most of the time our final determination isn't the least bit logical. We end up acting or reacting to issues based on conjecture.

### Natural Tendencies

As situations escalate negative voices in our heads kick in and our natural tendency is to assess guilt, place blame, or accept shame. Some people are quick to take responsibility for any incident whether they had control over it or not, and others assume no accountability when they should. Our inner child's feelings are wounded, or our inner adult rears its ugly head with indignation. A negative spiral begins that is almost impossible to reverse.

**Disconnected and Isolated**

Incidents accumulate, and over time they are blown entirely out of proportion. Huge arguments erupt, and relationships deteriorate. It happens in our marriages, with our children, our parents, and very frequently in the workplace. In the end, we feel disconnected and isolated, and often we disregard opportunities to rectify the situation. We erect walls that don't allow open and honest communication. Pent-up emotions cause us to either blow-up or clam-up. None of these actions resolve anything and only aggravate the situation.

**It's time for a change.**

## *The Guarantee*

How Can a Talking Stick Session Guarantee You Are Understood?
It's quite simple.

Someone, a speaker holding a talking stick, says what they would like to say. The listener must repeat what they understood to the speaker's satisfaction. If the speaker does not feel they were understood, they have the right to restate their position and the process repeats until the speaker feels they are understood. Then the stick is passed, and the listener becomes the speaker.

There's much more to the process, of course, but these are the basics.

## *The 10 Rules of Engagement*

1. **Talking Stick sessions ensure individuals an opportunity to speak their mind, be heard and guaranteed they're understood.**

   Rule 1 is the backbone of Talking Stick sessions, and the following nine rules describe the aspects that make the process one of the most powerful on the planet.

   **Promotes respect and boosts self-esteem.** Participants find sessions safe, relaxed spaces, free from judgment, criticism, and punishment. The 10 Rules of Engagement foster consideration, recognition, and appreciation of others and their opinions. When an individual receives respect from another, it automatically raises their self-esteem and may heal something inside them that has been lost or stolen.

   **Creates excellent listening skills.** Talking Sticks reveal the reasons we are generally such terrible listeners and show us how to become the type of listener we want listening to us.

2. **The environment of a Talking Stick should always be one of respect.**

   Sessions promote respect and should never be used to humiliate, disgrace, or humble another person. The ultimate demonstration of respect in a Talking Stick session occurs during the passing of the talking stick. When both the speaker and the designated listener are holding the stick they make eye contact, hold it for a second, nod slightly to acknowledge the connection and then release it to the receiving person. Many indigenous people say the eyes are the window to the soul. This eye-lock is called the Gift of Respect.

All of the Rules of Engagement foster respect if adhered to and there are numerous examples and suggested responses in Chapter 7 – Speaker and Listener Tips and Etiquette to help both sides rescue a session if it starts to go off course. Especially during the actual Guarantee process emotions can run high on both sides. A Talking Stick session is designed to help repair damaged relationships caused by poor or lack of communication and help us reconnect where we have become disconnected and isolated. They should give us the opportunity for an open, honest discussion if both sides remember to keep an attitude of respect.

See Chapter 1 - / Iroquois Confederacy and Our Founding Fathers
See Chapter 6 – /The Guarantee and Proper Passing Protocol
See Chapter 7 – Speaker and Listener Tips and Etiquette

3. **Whatever needs to be said can be said without worry of criticism or judgment.**

   This Rule requires both speakers and listeners to remain open-minded, remembering that all participants deserve to be heard and understood. You may be a listener now but will be a speaker soon. How do you want to be treated? Rule 2: The environment of a Talking Stick should always be one of respect, and Rule 7: All opinions are valid, is this rules backbone.

   There is a story about a young woman I encountered in a session I facilitated. The whole account is in Chapter 8 – Stories and Examples/The Fidgety Young Woman, but the gist is this woman was so fearful of being criticized by the other participants that she found herself being very judgmental toward everyone else said and was becoming more and more uncomfortable. During a break, I told her a story, and she went back in with the intent of being open to anything that was said, and immediately felt the uncomfortable pressure dissolve. When it was her turn to speak again, she realized everyone was receptive to what she had to say. It's a principle known in quantum physics called Likes Attract Likes. Whatever you fear, you attract. Fearing judgment, she felt judged. Thank goodness the universe is neutral. If you put out positive thoughts or vibrations, that's what you will invite.

If all participants intend to respect and understand the principle that everyone's view is based on their frame of reference and to them, it is perfectly valid, that's a good foundation for a Talking Stick session. The positive energy of the meeting can be enhanced even more when intentions are consciously set to be open-minded, to have a successful outcome, or to attract whatever is important to you or the highest good of the collective.

4. **All participants are equal.**

   In Chapter 1 – What is a Talking Stick? Where Did They Originate? I talked about the two traditions the Iroquois Confederacy believed kept them at peace for millennia. The first is Talking Stick sessions and the second is the structure of their Council of Elders.

   When the council met, they conducted sessions in a circle or wheel. There was no one at the head of a table or standing behind a podium as official meetings are lead today. The shape automatically leveled the playing field. Likely included was the Chief, a Shaman (Medicine Man/Woman), a War Chief and others that carried status among the people. In most traditions, the Chief was a spokesperson and leader only because he/she was charismatic, trusted, and a good organizer. Decisions affecting the whole tribe were rarely made by any of these individuals, but by the council.

A person's outside status carried no weight, but being a woman did. Assuming sixteen individuals participated, there would likely be seven men and nine women. A man and a woman would sit in each direction except in the west, which was considered the place reserved for the grandmothers. Two women would sit in the west giving the feminine viewpoint a definite advantage. Women were given the extra votes because they had twice as much to lose if the council voted for something dangerous, such as going to war. They ran the risk of losing both husbands and sons.

The tradition of equality continues within a Talking Stick session. Rule 7 states: All Opinions are valid. So, if all participants are equal and all opinions valid, then no one's idea is more important than another's. An individual agreeing to be a Talking Stick leader only means they decided to take on an additional job. It does not raise their status.

5. **A person can only speak when he or she has the talking stick.**

    When someone has the stick, others must refrain from talking, stating a different opinion, or interrupting in any way. It includes all gestures even ones indicating agreement, and especially when disagreeing with the speaker.

    In Chapter 6 – Planning Your Session, one of the topics is whether to allow notetaking in a session. Many designated listeners appreciate being allowed to jot down keywords to help them remember each point made by the speaker. It could help others plan what they want to include when it is their turn to speak. Notetaking is something that should be agreed to beforehand by all participants. If allowed, the notes should be brief. Someone with their head down writing continuously appears not to be listening, and this does not respect the speaker.

6. **Participants must always speak using "I" statements.**

    No one can speak for someone else unless all parties agree before the session begins. Speak for yourself and from the heart.

This rule eliminates most *he said/she said* arguments. The leader or facilitator should correct any party saying something like, "Bob said that Chloe said…" Unless a participant can say, "I heard Bob talking to Chloe…" it isn't an "I" statement.

If the participant didn't hear it, see it, touch it, smell it, or have feelings about it, it doesn't need to be part of a Talking Stick session.

7. **All opinions are valid.**

   We all have different belief systems. We were raised differently and had diverse backgrounds that influenced us. Even identical twins raised together have different frames of reference and believe their opinions are valid. As adults, one twin will remember a time when their father beat their mother or some other event, and the other will swear it didn't happen.

   When trying to discover the facts about a crime, law enforcement officials deal with inconsistency regularly. A man is shot and falls to the ground. Later, when interviewing witnesses, the first indicates the shooter came running from a specific direction wearing a black hoodie. The second witness recalls the involvement of two men, both having guns. He says that after the one with the brown zippered jacket shoots the victim, both run off into traffic. The first witness never saw the second man. A third witness is confident that the victim and shooter were walking together in business suits when suddenly one pulled a gun and shot the other.

   Our different opinions and belief systems whether we realize it or not were influenced by previous events in our lives and especially from early childhood. Actual events or the stories we told ourselves about events while trying to make sense of a situation, created our adult perspective on life.

   Conscientious listeners know that it may be easier to resolve a conflict if they understand how the other person gained their mindset or minimally what triggered the other person to feel the way they do currently. The listener will forego their ego and try to hear between the lines of the speaker's message. Of course, this is easier with a Personal-Family session, when something is known of the other person's history. In a business situation, rarely do we get to know the other party/parties well enough to go this deep. Generally, though, a desire to develop empathy is intuitively felt by the speaker resulting in the same positive results.

The Talking Stick process isn't meant to change anyone's opinion or belief, and the speaker or listener should never feel coerced to change, but many times listeners see a completely different perspective than they had before. The optimum result is for the listener to become more open-minded and cultivate respect for everyone's viewpoint.

See Chapter 7 – Walk in the Speaker's Shoes
See Chapter 8 – /Other Stories/There's Never Only One Way to Do Anything
See Chapter 8 – /Other Stories/Walking Around the Wheel

8. **Where a resolution is required, all participants should agree to resolve the issue for the highest good of all parties.**

In Conflict Resolution Talking Stick sessions, the purpose is always to find a solution in a matter of contention, and for a successful process it is essential for all parties to leave personal feelings at the door for this to happen.

At the beginning of Chapter 6 – Planning Your Session, I ask the question: Is a Talking Stick session appropriate for your group or topic? I ask because many times individuals agreeing to participate have different or ulterior motives not in alignment with the Rules of Engagement.

Here are several motives that I have run across:

* Looking for a safe place to start a fight.
* Wanting to embarrass or humiliate someone.
* Trying to please someone else.

A life coach I'd trained to be a facilitator encountered a man who was intimated by his sharp-tongued controlling wife. After the session the coach told me she believed he intended to have a *safe fight* with his wife; one where he could get a few words in, but she didn't think he had a genuine desire to resolve their issues.

In Chapter 8 I've included a lengthy story about a woman whose desire was to humiliate her husband. See the reference below.

I witnessed the third motive during a parent-teenager Personal-Family Talking Stick. The thirteen-year-old was getting counseling, but according to the therapist, they weren't making progress in changing her belief that her parent's recent divorce had nothing to do with her. Her father had moved out of the family home, and during weekends spent with him, the girl had started serving him like she was his slave. Her parents asked for a Talking Stick with the intent of persuading her that they'd divorced because they wanted different things in life and that she'd had nothing to with the breakup. But during the session, it was apparent that the young girl had only agreed in desperation to find one more way to please her father and try to get him to come home.

To get a resolution, participants need a *team approach*. A solution that is in the highest good for all parties requires an attitude and willingness to acquiesce and cooperate, sometimes ignoring personal perspectives or feelings.

See Chapter 8 – /Other Stories/Ulterior Motives Revealed

9. **Participants will never receive discipline as a direct result of something that is said or revealed during a Talking Stick.**

   Without this rule, there would be no reason for individuals to speak openly and honestly in some cases. A plaguing guilty conscious might give someone incentive to confess and get the issue off their chest, but many of us live entirely in denial. Subconsciously we feel, If it's secret, it's not real. When disclosed and discussed its undeniable, and that is something we aren't likely to do.

   After a confession, it is quite okay to discuss a punishment that would be enacted at a future time if specific actions, behaviors, or conduct continues, such as *I appreciate you telling your mother and I the truth about the dent in the fender. You have one speeding ticket. If you get a second or have any other accidents, you will lose car privileges for six months.* If a party sincerely confesses, shows remorse, asks for forgiveness, or states that it will never happen again, there should be some latitude.

   Be proactive as much as possible. For example, with the situation above parents can almost expect something like this to happen if they have a sixteen-year-old with a new driver's license. If taken off guard, it would be a normal reaction for them to scream at the teenager, with their first thought being fear for the teen's safety and then thinking about the cost of the repair. Having a private discussion about how the teenager should be dealt with if a particular situation arises (especially after the first traffic ticket) could keep session rational.

10. **What is said within a Talking Stick session is never discussed with anyone outside the original Talking Stick participants.**

    Before a session begins, especially if someone is new to the process, review the 10 Rules of Engagement. All parties must agree about sharing or discussing information with anyone who is not one of the original participants. Rule 10 can be considered a continuation of Rule 9. For someone to speak openly and honestly, he or she may need to know the information will go no further than the other party or participants in the group.

There are times when decisions made during a session could hurt more than repair past damage if those decisions, or the process of making the decisions, is divulged to an outsider. Trying to convey emotions and sentiments of a session is very difficult, and the outsider may completely misconstrue what happened. In most cases, Talking Stick sessions are best kept confidential.

# Chapter 3
# Dad and the "D" Grade
## Actual Personal/Family Talking Stick Example

Mr. Swanson heard giggling as the front door swung open and his son and football star, Derik, came through with his arm around his girlfriend, Samantha.

"Dad, this is a surprise. I didn't expect you home from work so early," said Derik.

"Life is full of surprises today, Derik. I didn't expect Samantha to be with you. Hi, Sam," answered Mr. Swanson. "I expected you to be coming home to study. I believe that's what you said you were going to do this morning."

Mr. Swanson thought the world of Samantha. If a father could wish for a perfect daughter-in-law, it would be her; he just hoped it would be four or five years away and after college.

Mr. Swanson continued, "My first surprise was Ms. Nelson's call giving me a heads up that she was on her way to Coach Tyler to tell him you'd gotten another "D" on your Chem Test. It doesn't look like you're playing in the game Friday night. Had you heard?"

"No." Derik lost all his swagger and crumpled into the nearest chair.

"Sam," said Mr. Swanson, "The weather is nice. Can you walk home, or do you need a ride? Derik and I need an official discussion about these grades. I believe a Talking Stick is in order. He doesn't seem to be taking this seriously."

"I'm fine. I'll see you tomorrow, Derik." Sam made a hasty retreat.

"Well, glad everyone is fine," said Mr. Swanson, as the door clicked shut. "We've done this often enough, although we aren't planning our vacation this time. I believe this process will be a Fact Finding session. I've thought about it. "What needs to be done to get your grades up?" I'm asking for the Talking Stick, so you get to choose the time and place."

"Okay, Dad. Let me grab a protein bar and let's go out on the patio."

Mr. Swanson initiated the session, so he is the first to speak. He held the talking stick with both hands and looked his son in the eye.

**Mr. Swanson as speaker:** As I said inside, I open this Talking Stick because I need some answers. I don't want to force you into anything. Your mother and I raised you to make up your mind, and up to this point, you've said it was your dream to play ball at a Big Ten school and you know to do that you have to get a scholarship. Your grades have been slipping since the middle of last year and Chemistry this year has been a disaster. What does this mean?

Mr. Swanson nodded slightly as a signal to Derik that he was finished speaking and ready for Derik to start the Guarantee step.

**Derik as designated listener:** What I understood you to say was that it's my decision, but if it is still my dream to play football at a Big Ten school, I have to take my grades a lot more seriously and get a scholarship. And, you want to know what's happened since last year to cause my grades to drop and especially what's going on with Chemistry. Right?

Derik made eye contact with his dad, who was still holding the stick in his lap, both of his hands close to the ends. Mr. Swanson nodded indicating that he felt he was understood and leaned forward to present the stick to his son. After meeting his dad's eyes and holding the contact for a second or two, Derik grasped the stick using both hands toward the middle and nodded in return. His dad released the staff, and Derik became the speaker.

**Derik as speaker:** (after several deep breaths to ground himself) You're right. Since last year, I guess I have let things slide. (he came on with a rush) It all happened so fast. I met Sam and won those awards, Penn State and Michigan were interested in me and, well, life was perfect. When I got the first "D," I couldn't admit I wasn't perfect. I think you call it denial. I know what I promised. I never thought it could come to this. I hope I haven't destroyed my dream of college football. I've let you down.

Derik raced through the last of this, and Mr. Swanson could see that his son was getting choked up, so he gestured with his hands to indicate he was ready to take the stick back. Derik glanced up and pushed the stick forward relieved. Mr. Swanson began the Guarantee step.

**Mr. Swanson as designated listener:** What I understood you to say was that everything was going so great for you that you let your ego run amuck and you didn't want to think that your grades could slip. What you never imagined was that anything could keep you off the field and you feel you've let me down. You still have the dream of playing college ball. Is that about it?

Still sitting in a posture indicating the weight of the world on his shoulders, Derik nodded, and he reversed the passing process giving the stick back to his father. Mr. Swanson was now the speaker.

**Mr. Swanson as speaker:** The first thing I want to say is that you haven't let me down; you've let yourself down. At this point in your life, you are almost a man. I believe I've taught you about all I can. Now it's my job to nudge you back into the middle of the road occasionally, and then it's your decision. The second thing is that I believe we all have egos that we need to check from time to time and learn how to channel that energy into positive self-esteem but stay humble. That's something you must figure out. Third, if you're ready to keep your promises, I believe I know a guy who can tutor you in

Chemistry. I don't think you need tutoring on any other subject if you buckle down and get serious. These changes will probably mean some sacrifice, and I will leave you to decide what that means."

**Derik as designated listener:** (with a much lighter demeanor) What I understood you to say was we need good self-esteem and have to keep our egos in check at the same time and that I have to figure out how to do that. You said if I'd promise to bring my other grades back up that you'd get me a Chem tutor and that would be great (he rolled his eyes). And, you are sure I'll have to make sacrifices.

Derik looked over like he was ready to take the stick, but Mr. Swanson stopped him.

**Mr. Swanson as speaker:** You missed something. I also said that you hadn't let me down, you'd let yourself down.

**Derik as designated listener:** Got it. What I understood you to say was that I hadn't let you down, but that I had let myself down.

Mr. Swanson nodded and held out the stick. Derik continued to make eye contact with his dad.

**Derik as speaker:** You have my promise, Dad. You'll start seeing lots of better grades. I know I can get "A's" again. I really, really need that tutor though. I just don't get Chemistry. Are we done? I need to make a phone call.

**Mr. Swanson:** (Mr. Swanson chuckled) Yes, we can close this Talking Stick.

Mr. Swanson sat on the patio a few minutes longer wondering if his son would have the same self-esteem and family respect if he and his wife hadn't started raising the kids to make their own choices and decisions and guided them with the use of a Talking Stick since they were four or five years old. He didn't think so. He'd talked to too many other parents.

He heard his wife's car in the drive. When he went in to greet her, he overheard Derik on the phone with Sam. "Well, we can still eat lunch together every day and grab some pizza after the game on Friday, it's just I have to come home right after practice and study every day. We can't hang out as much till I get my grades up."

# Chapter 4
# Splitting the Group
## Actual Organization/Business Talking Stick Example with Multiple Segments

**The History**

I pulled into Chris' drive and saw her sitting on the front porch. She didn't need to say a word; her body language told me something was terribly wrong. The first words out of her mouth were, "Greg is having an affair with Pat."

"What? That's the craziest thing I ever heard. You've got to be joking. Pat and Greg? They're about as different as apples and oran... avocados," I said.

I couldn't believe my ears. My eyes shifted two doors down to the gray house where Pat lived, had lived with Tim, her husband, until two weeks ago. Pat and I had been friends since college until a few months back when she started acting strangely. We'd talked about everything under the sun for years, but not marital problems. Then suddenly she announced she was leaving Tim and moved out overnight. Ten years ago, Chris and Greg had bought their house on Franklin, and the four had been almost inseparable couple-friends since. According to them, there'd been no warning either. I'd called Pat several times, but she'd acted distracted and just kept saying she'd call me back. Right then it dawned on me that she never had.

Pat came from wealthy parents, loved to eat at gourmet restaurants on the Country Club Plaza and shop at Sacs Fifth Ave where I just tagged along and dreamed. Even as a best friend, I had to say that snooty was a proper adjective for her. Tim, the husband that Pat had just left, was a dry-humored fireman and football fanatic that everyone loved. He was the life of every party. Quiet described Greg, Chris' husband. He was a country boy, contractor, fisherman, and sports enthusiast. Chris wasn't country, but not Country Club Plaza either. I hadn't known her near as well as Pat until the last few months. Now, we were becoming best friends. I was more outgoing, and she was more family-centric. But from the short time we'd been close, I'd use dry-humored and loyal to describe her. With their similar humor, I would have matched Chris and Tim way before I would have considered Pat and Greg. This whole scenario was mindboggling.

"Are you sure it's an affair? Have you got proof?" I asked.

As Chris raised her head, the dam broke, and tears streamed down her cheeks. "Last week, Greg didn't come home after work till late several times and I drove by Pat's new apartment. His car was out front. He didn't come home at all last night, and it was there at 7:30 this morning when I dropped the girls at the sitter. And, she's not answering her phone. I've felt him being strange for a couple of months but couldn't put the finger on it. I thought maybe it was work."

I stood there dazed having no idea what to say until Mariah and Sierra, Chris and Greg's two little granddaughters ran out the front door welcoming me. Mariah was four, and Sierra was two and a half.

I picked up Sierra and turned away from Chris to give her space to collect herself. "Hey, girl, on my way over here I got a craving for ice cream. I know you love ice cream, but I don't think Mariah does. What should we do if she won't go?" Within seconds I was on my knees in the grass and had succumbed to the mobbing. We made it to Baskin Robbins without more discussion.

I'd bought a new house several months before and wanted French doors between the great room and stone patio. Greg had promised to install them. He showed up Saturday as promised at 10:00 am. Pat showed up at 10:30. When I opened the door, my mouth fell open. She walked past me and came in like she always had. An elephant followed her into the room, but neither of us acknowledged it. We stood in the kitchen and chatted never mentioning Chris or Greg.

After about ten minutes the conversation lagged, and she headed for the great room and curled up in a big chair to watch Greg work on the doors. I couldn't force myself to go into the room. I fabricated an excuse and found some work I had to do in my office and made a quick exit. I could hear them talking off and on, but not what they said. The doorbell rang again at noon and Pat, and I ran into each other heading to the door. It was the Domino's Pizza man.

"I thought everyone was probably getting hungry," said Pat. "I got three mediums; a white chicken something for me, pepperoni and hot sausage for you, and a MeatZZa™ for Greg. I know he loves Dominos MeatZZa™."

Words couldn't describe how uncomfortable I felt, and I just stared at her and said the first thing that popped into my mind, "And, how would you know that?"

She mumbled something about having been friends for years, paid the guy and then headed back to the great room carrying the boxes without meeting my eye. I'd had enough. I stood there telling myself not to do anything rash, and then followed. The elephant had gotten so large I was suffocating.

The old sliding doors were gone, and Greg was standing half in/half out measuring when I said, "I don't know what you guys are doing, but you aren't going to do it in my house. I may end up with a huge hole in my wall because I don't know what you are going to do, Greg, but Pat, you have to leave."

She did, without a word. Greg stayed and finished the job. At 4:30 he stuck his head in my office and said he was through except for needing more trim for the outside. He would get that and put it up this coming week. I was going to do the painting and staining, so that was that. Thank goodness his work was impeccable. There wasn't much else to say. I sincerely thanked him and wrote him a check.

I called Chris later and told her the story. She didn't sound surprised. She'd confronted Greg the night before, but he hadn't admitted anything, just left. The next day was Mother's Day. We never knew whether he was aware of what day it was or not. He showed up while Chris was making their usual Sunday waffle breakfast and quietly told her he wanted a divorce.

One of the things that Pat and I had been involved in together was a women's group that met monthly for socials, charity projects, and camaraderie. Chris had never shown any desire to be part of the group, and that was one of the reasons we'd never become close, though I had known her for a long time. About the same time that I felt Pat changing, she also started coaxing Chris to join in events with the group. As Chris became a regular, everyone began to enjoy her sense of humor, but I could tell she wasn't doing it for herself, but for Pat. Our monthly meeting was coming up the Thursday after Mother's Day and I realized we might have a situation on our hands. I called Pat and asked if she was planning to go. Her answer shocked me.

She said, "No, I've been planning to leave the group for a long time. You can tell everyone at the meeting that I won't be back. I knew Greg was going to divorce Chris and that's why I've been getting her involved. I knew she would be devastated and need something to occupy her time."

"Occupy her time?" I said. Pat had commented like she was talking about knitting an afghan. "How long have you and Greg been doing this?"

"Well, we've known for years, but we've only been sleeping together for about six months."

"And, you've been planning what's best for Chris for some time now?" I asked.

Chris didn't need coaxing to stay home from the Thursday meeting. I asked the president if I could have a few minutes to tell the group what I knew of Chris and Greg's split and that Tim was leaving. She put me on the agenda. I had decided to omit the gory details about moving on Mother's Day and the fact that Pat had been planning this for some time. When I arrived, I discovered Pat had been on the phone with several members, and there were already several different stories going around. The group began to shatter and split that night. Pat was gone, and even though it was her plan, several members were missing her already. Several of us convinced Chris that we loved her and wanted her to remain part of the organization. She continued and became more involved than before even going through the initiation. Pat's plan was working. Tension subsided among the women until the end of the year.

Greg quit construction and took a job with a large national chain of hunting and fishing stores, which forced him to work in a city three hours away. He was only going to be home a few times a month. Pat showed up at our group's meeting and announced she'd changed her mind and wanted to come back. Timing was neither Pat's nor Greg's strong suit. The event she chose was our Holiday Party. She had a gift for everyone as if that would make everything *right with the world*. Chris exited silently within minutes of Pat's entrance, and the president guided Pat to the door before she was done portraying Santa Claus. Instead of enjoying the Santa Steal the Present game, the room erupted into a chaotic discussion of what to do. Merry Christmas to all!

Most of the women knew I'd spent eight years as a shamanic apprentice while I lived in Colorado and California. I'd received training from several amazing Native American elders. My formal training ended in 2004, and I'd continued sharing the wisdom in many forms with others, but at that point, I'd never done anything with these women. One ceremonial process that I learned was how to facilitate *Talking Sticks*. I wouldn't publish the first version of this book, *The Talking Stick: Guarantee You Are Understood and Not Just Heard* until 2010, but right now seemed like a good time to step forward and start sharing with these women.[3]

## The Talking Stick Session

Between Christmas and New Year's, I met with the officers and described a Talking Stick process and told them I would lead it. They agreed we would need to vote, but no one had a better idea to try and salvage the group.

Chapter 5 – Types of Talking Sticks discusses the six basic types of Talking Stick sessions, and it appeared we might need to combine four out of the six: Welcoming, Fact Finding, Difficult Discussions, and Conflict Resolution for our process.

An email went out describing the process, including the Rules of Engagement and what the Guarantee entailed. The first step was to decide what we wanted to accomplish. The Holiday Party had run the gamut from welcome Pat back like the prodigal son with a fatted calf to stone her in the village square. And, where did Chris fit?

A majority voted to have a Talking Stick session. At the time we had 15 members, which included Chris, but not Pat. Three stated they did not want to participate but stipulated they would go along with the group's decision. Two of those, Sonja and Celest, were interested in the process and agreed to be a timer and recorder. Chris refused to come but wrote a letter for me to read to the group. Pat had no problem being present.

---

[3] See the Prologue or Appendix B – Guarantee You Are Understood Initiative

**Win-Win or Lose-Lose**

I kept going back to the 9th Rule of Engagement: Participants will never receive discipline as a direct result of something that is said or revealed during a Talking Stick. I felt I was violating this rule. In reality, we weren't. Pat was asking for reinstatement and if the group voted *no* that wasn't punishment. If the group voted her back, then it would be Chris' choice to decide what to do; I couldn't construe that as punishment. Was it fair? I wasn't sure there was anything fair about this debacle.

I presented my ideas for the scope of the event, and even though I would have liked to make a recommendation on the voting process, as acting leader, my job was to be impartial. I felt it fair though that the officers decided that at least a two-thirds majority would be needed to reinstate Pat.

This was the agenda we can up with:

- Welcoming session – Phyllis opens and gives brief instructions – the purpose of Talking Stick – state names for the record – practice passing protocol and Guarantee step.
- Close Welcoming.

- Change type to Fact Finding with Q&A Combo format.
- Phyllis opens and gives instructions.
- Pat (Candidate) first speaker and answers all questions.
- Popcorn style and everyone gets two pitches.
- Phyllis reads Chris' letter.

- Close Fact Finding.
- Pat leaves the wheel and room.
- 15-Minute Break.

- Change type to Conflict Resolution.
- Phyllis opens and gives instructions.
- Popcorn style for comments, three-minute timed, everyone gets one pitch.
- Circle style, one round for voting.
- Close Conflict Resolution.

- Change type to Difficult Discussion.
- Pat brought back in.
- Phyllis opens and gives instructions.
- Pat informed of group's decision.
- Popcorn style for comments and reflections, three-minute timed, one pitch.
- Close Difficult Discussion.

- Close Talking Stick.

Typically, our meetings rotated between member's homes, but to follow Talking Stick protocol I looked for a neutral location. The president of the group was a high school teacher and said using her classroom on a Saturday would be fine. We gathered at 9:00 am.

I had the classroom set up, so it looked like the diagram on the next page. Everyone's had a chair facing in. As Recorder, Sonja's job was to turn on the recorder, state the name of each type of session as they changed, i.e., Welcoming and then let it run till the end. Celest's job didn't start until the Conflict Resolution round. She had two phones. One was set for 2 minutes 45 seconds and the other for 15 seconds. When a speaker began, she would start the 2 minutes 45-second timer. When it ran out, she would let it chime for two beats and make sure the speaker heard, stop it, and then punch the 15-second phone to give them time to wrap up. If they didn't wrap up after 15 seconds, she was to stand up to let me know time was out.

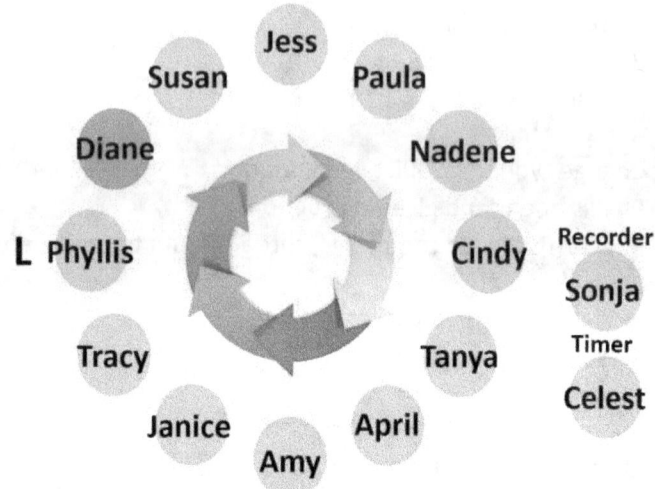

**Welcoming Session**

Phyllis as leader: Thanks everyone for coming. I know that for most of you Talking Stick sessions are new, so if you are confused or have any questions, please speak up, but of course, don't interrupt any of the other participants while they are speaking. I'll be asking you some questions to make sure you understand the process, and you only need to answer if you disagree or need more clarification. To keep it simple, if you agree, you don't have to say anything. Okay? (silence) Great, either you are catching on quickly, or I have you completely intimidated.

Pat has asked to rejoin our group, and so her reinstatement is the purpose for the entire Talking Stick. There will be four rounds, and I will explain them and give instructions as we go along.

I have agreed to lead the process. Leadership requires that I be familiar with Talking Stick etiquette, the Rules of Engagement, and be impartial in running the session, but I may express my own opinion while I hold the talking stick, or when I am the designated listener.

We're going to start with a Welcoming round. The desired result is two-fold and very simple. I'm going to state my name for the record and Sonja is going to record our session today. So, question 1 – Is there anyone who objects to being recorded? (silence) Okay. The second part of the desired result is to make sure everyone understands the talking stick passing protocol and the Guarantee process because we are going to be using this over and over today.

I'll start and that makes me the speaker. You probably read in the email that went out that in a Talking Stick session the speaker is always guaranteed to be understood. We accomplish that by having a designed listener repeat what they perceived the speaker to say. If the speaker feels understood, then the stick is passed to the listener, and the listener becomes the next speaker. The style of Talking Stick we are starting with is called circular, which means that the designated listener is on my left, Pat that's you. As a speaker you always want to make sure your listener hears you, so as I hold the talking stick, I'm going to face you and state my name for the record.

**Phyllis as speaker:** Phyllis Cronbaugh.

Now I am ready to see if you were listening. I indicate that I am prepared to pass by nodding slightly, but I still hold the stick with both my hands.

As the designated listener you always start your reply with, "What I understood you to say was..." So, Pat?

**Pat as designated listener:** What I understood you to say was that your name was Phyllis Cronbaugh.

**Phyllis as speaker:** Great. If I feel that you truly understood me, I nod or acknowledge that in some way and continue passing the stick to you. The actual protocol for passing is this:

When passing the talking stick, hold it with both hands close to the ends and present it to the other person. Wait for them to grasp the middle using both of their hands. Make eye contact and hold it for a second, nod slightly and when they have responded release the stick to them.

Does everyone have that? We'll practice as it goes around. So, Pat, you are now the speaker and Susan you are the designated listener. Take it away.

*I completed the round when I acted as the designated listener for Tracy.*

**Phyllis as leader:** We achieved our desired result, which was to state our names and become familiar with the passing process, so I close this phase of our Talking Stick.

**Fact Finding Session**

**Phyllis as leader:** Everyone needs additional instruction for this round. I gave you extensive information on the Rules of Engagement in the email that went out. Are there questions?

**Susan with question:** I know I'm supposed to be speaking for myself in "I" statements, but I think number 7 about judgment is going to be very hard for all of us. I keep going back and telling myself to have an open mind, but I know I don't. I'm going to have to hear something very convincing here today to get me to change my mind.

**Phyllis as leader:** Well, you are honest Susan and aware that you want to keep an open mind. I believe that is the first step. Someone who thinks they have an open mind when it's shut very tight isn't in reality.

**Tanya with question:** Number 10 says that we must keep what's said confidential; we never discuss what happens in a Talking Stick with anyone outside the original group. Does that include Joan, who couldn't make it today?

Phyllis as Leader: Pat, you will not be present during the Conflict Resolution segment of the session. I want to make sure we enforce Rule 10 during that time, but it is your decision concerning Joan. Do you want to vote?

(yes) Okay. Pat, you need to abstain and Celest and Sonja, I think you should be allowed to vote. In almost all voting in a Talking Stick it takes a two-thirds majority to pass, so that means we will need eight votes. All in favor of sharing what was said today with Joan if she asks, raise your hand. (counting – 7) Opposed (counting – 6). The vote has not carried. Please do not speak of what is said here today with anyone who is not present here in this room today. Any other questions?

Let's move on to speaker and listener etiquette.

When you are the speaker, take a second or two once you have the stick to ground yourself. You should make eye contact with the person you will converse with or the group as much as possible, but don't let it get theatrical. Never do anything that can be construed as drama or trying to stir up the pot. Remember, we have all come together with an attitude of respect.

As the leader, if I feel someone is doing something distracting, like exaggerating a great deal and either the speaker or designated listener is not coping with the situation in a reasonable manner, I will step in. The same goes for attitude, either verbal or body language, etc. If it happens and I feel I need to mention it, don't take it personally that is my job today as your leader.

This particular Fact Finding round uses a structure called Q&A Combo. Its origin is a political debate orientation, where someone is questioned, so officially today, you are Candidate Pat, and we'll direct all our questions or comments to you.

At this time, I officially change our purpose to a Fact Finding round and get going. As you all know Pat left last May, sorry, to talk like you aren't in the room, Pat, so, our desired result for this process is to understand why you left and why you want to come back and join us at this time. This is the complete scope of this round. There may be other issues that you would like Pat to clarify, but you will need to contact Pat about those things outside this session. Pat, you can certainly explain your actions and where you are coming from, but this is not the place for a discussion of the reasons for your divorce or future. (affirmative nods)

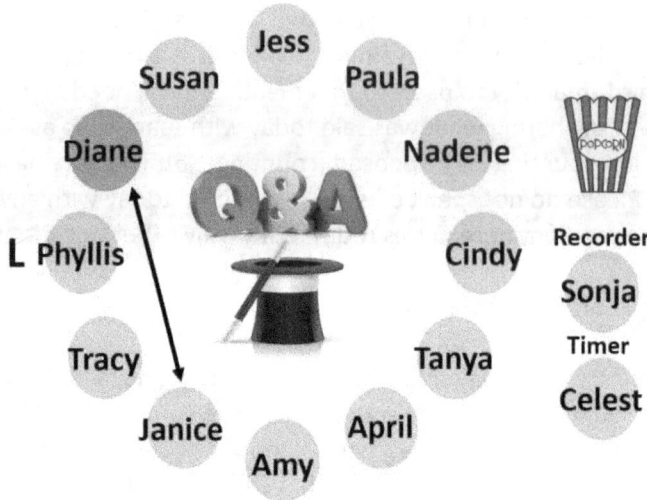

Questions about being the speaker?

**April's question:** Well, since we can't speak for anyone but ourselves, what about Chris? She's not here.

**Phyllis as leader:** That's true. You can only speak in "I" statements. Chris chose not to come today, and the officers and I agreed to let her write a letter that I will read to everyone when you are complete with your questions to Pat. So, she will have a voice.

And, that reminds me. The rotation of the stick is different this time, and we will pass a little differently too. The style this time is called popcorn style, which means that when Pat is finished giving her initial remarks, she will place the talking stick in the middle of the wheel in the top hat. Anyone may come forward and accept it. When you do, you become the designated listener just like we did in the Welcoming session. You repeat to Pat what you understood and when she feels complete you become the speaker and ask your question or give your comments.

The passing of the stick is different because the speaker, Pat in this case, has relinquished the talking stick when she put it in the middle of the circle. When the designated listener picks it up, they hold it during the time they accomplish the Guarantee.

You have two chances to speak, or pitch as we call it, or you don't have to at all if you don't want to. When no one else takes the stick, I will be the designated listener and complete the final Guarantee, and this part of the Fact Finding round will end.

Okay? It's a lot to take in, I know. Once you have done it, it will start to become logical. (everyone agreed)

Those are tips for speakers. As the designated listener, you have the most significant duty of anyone here; you accomplish the Guarantee, which is the heart of a Talking Stick session.

I'm speaking in general, so no one takes offense. Stay in the present while you listen to the speaker. Let bygones be bygones. Try to keep an open mind. You all know what "walk in someone else's shoes" means. Well, walk in the speaker's shoes, which is more than listening. Try to discern why they feel the way they do. It doesn't mean you are going to change your view, but when you perceive why they have the opinion they do, you may have more respect for them. Remember, all opinions are valid. Everyone has the right to their perspective.

Always begin with, "What I understood you to say was…" and then proceed with what you believe the speaker intended. Now, for the rest of you, if you hear the designated listener repeat something that isn't what you understood the speaker to say, feel free to bring it up and get clarification. Questions?

**Paula question:** What if we don't get it right?

**Phyllis as leader:** Well, the speaker is going to let you know what you missed or that you didn't understand their intention and you get to try again. You get to keep going until you get it right. That's the Guarantee. I told you beforehand that you could bring paper into the circle to take brief notes. Just keywords. This is not the time to write out responses to what the speaker has said. Okay? (silence)

We are ready to begin. Pat?

*Phyllis completes the pass to Pat.*

*It was easy to see that Pat was a bit overwhelmed. I felt for her. She sat among women she had called friends for years and now only knew where a few of them stood on her situation. She'd been so closed-mouthed with me before she made her announcement, I wondered if she'd confided in anyone. I watched, and she took a deep breath and pulled herself up, looked at each person around the wheel, and was ready to speak.*

**Candidate Pat as speaker:** I'm not sure where to start. I know you have questions. All I can say now is that I realize I just slipped out of all your lives without any explanation. I'm sorry about that. If I had it to do all over again, I would do it differently. I made some decisions I'm sorry for. (she glanced at me) I guess I will let you ask the questions. So, I just put the stick in the hat?

**Phyllis as leader:** Yes.

*Pat walks to the center and places the stick in the black top hat. Janice is the first to come forward. She removes the talking stick and goes back to her seat then looks across the circle meeting Pat's eyes.*

**Janice as designated listener:** What I heard you say, Pat, was…

**Phyllis as leader:** Janice, hold on a minute, did you understand what Pat said or did you just hear her?

**Janice as designated listener:** Sorry. Pat, what I *understood* you to say was that you slipped out of all our lives without an explanation when you left and if you had it to do over you would do it differently. You are sorry about some of the decisions you made. (Pat nods yes)

**Phyllis as leader:** So, you agree that Janice understood you, Pat? (Pat nods again) Okay. Then we can say that Janice, as the designated listener has accomplished the Guarantee and Janice, you are now the speaker. It's essential for the two of you to do an eye lock before you begin speaking, Janice like you would have if Pat were handing you the stick. Indigenous people say the eyes are windows to the soul and making eye contact keeps the element of respect.

**Janice as speaker:** Okay. Well, none of what you did seems *spur of the moment* to me. I feel it's something you planned for a long time without telling anyone and since the group is so close, that hurts me more than the fact that you left. I've shared a lot of secrets with this group, and I would like to think that the group loves me as much as I love all of you, and I don't believe you showed any of us love or respect.

*Tears were starting to roll down Janice's cheeks, so I grabbed the box of tissues I'd remembered to bring and handed them to her. Experience told me we were going to need them today.*

**Phyllis as leader:** Okay, I need to interrupt again. Sorry, Janice. Everyone can probably say they have injured feelings. The officers set our purpose, and we can't deviate into personal issues. I need to keep us on track. The questions or comments made today are only to be about why Pat left last May and why she wishes reinstatement. We aren't going to get into how each of us feels we were hurt, etc. Okay? Janice, do you have an actual question for Pat?

**Janice as speaker:** Yes. Why did you leave? Tanya and Mike divorced three years ago, and she didn't go. I believe she felt the group supported her through the tough times. That's it.

*Janice places the stick in the top hat.*

**Candidate Pat as designated listener:** I'm the listener now? (I nod) May I take one minute to answer the first part of Janice's question? I won't take more than a minute.

*I glanced at Nadene, who was our current president. No one on a wheel is supposed to be more important than another. My status as leader didn't give me any authority to make decisions other than keeping us on track and ensuring everyone follow protocol and the Rules of Engagement. Nadene's official status meant nothing inside the wheel either, but she nodded imperceptibly and so I indicated it was okay.*

**Candidate Pat as designated listener:** Thank you. Do I do the Guarantee thing? (I nodded yes) Okay, what I understood you to say, Janice was that you felt I had been planning to leave for a long time and had never told anyone, and the fact that I'd been keeping secrets from the group was more hurtful than me quitting. I believe you're saying that you would never do that and feel that if we all love each other, we'd be relying on each other for support instead of bailing out. Is that good? (Janice nods yes)

**Candidate Pat as speaker:** I will say that last May I felt invincible and that I didn't need anyone anymore. At my age, you would think I would know better. Of course, those times didn't last. I believe I was a coward and couldn't face all of you, probably from a fear of being judged. Okay. Janice, your last question. My situation was different than Tanya's. I think all of you know now that I left Tim to be with Greg, who I love very much, and I knew it was going to be very awkward for me to be part of the group with Chris in it. I didn't see how that would work.

*Pat placed the stick in the top hat. I watched Cindy across the wheel from me as Pat made her last comment. She leaped out of her chair and headed for the stick.*

**Cindy as designated listener:** We're done with the first part now, right? Can I just do the last question? (I indicated yes) Pat, what I understood you to say was that your situation was different than Tanya's when she and Mike split up. Of course, that's true. Mike ran off with his secretary, and you ran off with another member of our group's ...

**Phyllis as leader:** Cindy, hold on. You are not the speaker yet. First, you must complete the Guarantee to Pat's satisfaction. She needs to feel understood.

**Cindy as designated listener:** Yeah, I got carried away. Pat, what I understood you to say was that your situation was different than Tanya's because you were now with another member of our group's husband and you felt it was going to be awkward to stay. Right? (Pat nods in agreement)

**Cindy as speaker:** I can see how your situation was different, Pat. The part of your last comment that bothers me the most is that you said it was going to be, and I quote, very awkward for *you to be part of the group* with Chris in it. Embarrassing for you? Was it going to be awkward for Chris? Was it going to be awkward for the rest of us? That's my question.

*Cindy placed the stick in the top hat and sat down. Pat hesitated and then moved forward.*

**Phyllis as leader:** I know this is an emotional Talking Stick, but I need to remind everyone that the second Rule of Engagement states: The environment of a Talking Stick should always be one of respect. Is everyone in agreement? (Nods of agreement)

**Candidate Pat as designated listener:** What I understood you to say Cindy is that you get that my situation is different than Tanya's and that my saying being part of the group along with Chris would be awkward for me. Is that right? (Cindy nods in agreement)

**Candidate Pat as speaker:** I certainly didn't mean that it would only be awkward for me. Of course, it would be uncomfortable for everyone. Sorry, for my poor choice of words.

*Pat places the stick in the top hat, and Susan moves to accept it.*

**Susan as designated listener:** Pat what I understood you to say is that you are sorry for your poor choice of words and that you felt it would be awkward for everyone. (Pat nods)

**Susan as speaker:** Pat, we've been friends for a long time. I guess what I want to know is why you have decided to come back. Why now and what's changed. If you come back, it's still going to be awkward.

*Susan places the stick in the hat and Pat retrieves it.*

**Candidate Pat as designated listener:** What I understood you to say was that we've been friends for a long time, and you want to know why I've decided I'd like to rejoin the group now, what's changed, and that you want me to see that it's still going to be awkward. (Susan agrees)

**Candidate Pat as speaker:** Well, Greg has taken a job in Springfield, and he will probably only be back two or three times a month for a couple of days. Just the thought of this has made me realize how much I've missed all of you and your friendship. I would like to rekindle those relationships.

*Pat puts the talking stick in the top hat, and no one moves for a minute. Finally, Amy gets up.*

**Amy as designated listener:** Pat, what I understood you to say was that Greg is taking a job in Springfield and he will only be back here a few times a month. In the time since you left the group, you've realized how much your women friends meant to you, and you want to get those friendships going again. Have I understood you? (Pat nods)

**Amy as speaker:** (Pause) I thought I had something to say, but I think I want that *pass on your time to speak* as you called it.

**Phyllis as leader:** *Pass on your right to speak*. You almost had it. LOL Would anyone else like to come forward and take the stick?

*No one else comes forward.*

Okay, then I am going to end this part of the Fact Finding round. The part that is remaining is to read the letter that Chris sent us. Are you all ready? I tore open the envelope.

Dear Friends,

I've never been a joiner. Several years ago, if someone would have told me that I was going to be a member of a group of women that were to mean as much to me as all of you do, I would have said they were nuts.

I know bonds strengthen when we face challenges in life and show up for each other. You were there for me and will always hold a special place in my heart for every one of you. The group as a whole and what it stands for means the world to me too. I don't know how this will turn out, but this group does so much good in the community and for each other that I know it must continue as a strong unit. I need to make it clear that I would have a tough time knowing that I was part of the reason for the group to split up. So, at this time, I need to say that I am leaving the group. I hope this makes it easier for you to do what you need to do.

With love in my heart, I hope to keep great friendships with each of you. You know where I live and there will always be a bottle of Merlot on my shelf along with a couple of glasses waiting.

Chris

*Several women were shocked. Pat didn't say a word.*

**Phyllis as leader:** The desired result for this Fact Finding segment was for everyone to ask Pat questions and hear Chris' letter. Everyone passed on their right to speak, and I have read the letter, so I believe we achieved this.

Pat, our next segment is called Conflict Resolution, and we ask that you wait outside for us. When we are complete with that round, we would like for you to rejoin us. (Pat nods)

At this time, let's take a fifteen-minute break. During the break, grab something to drink and stretch your legs. It's probably better if you didn't talk about the session. Thanks. See you back in fifteen minutes.

## *Conflict Resolution Session*

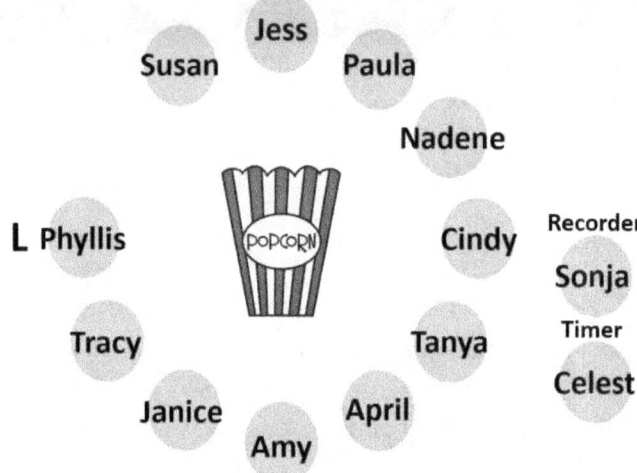

**Phyllis as leader:** This segment is now officially changed to a Conflict Resolution. In the last round, our desired result was to get the facts, ask questions, hear Pat's side of the story, and read Chris' letter so we could make an informed decision about whether to reinstate Pat as a member of our group. The desired result for this round changes to determining whether we will restore Pat as a member or not based on the knowledge we now have.

In this part, we have a chance to pitch our opinion one time for no more than three minutes in the same popcorn style so if you pick up the talking stick be ready to act as the designated listener. The difference in this round is that you are speaking to the group and not just to Pat. When everyone has pitched, or you have all passed on your right to speak, we will go around once more in a circular style taking a vote. There's no Guarantee step on a voting round; we pass the stick as we did during the Welcoming round and Sonja will record our votes. If you didn't get all that, I will guide you along.

Rule 10 states: What is said within a Talking Stick session is never discussed with anyone outside the original Talking Stick participants. Even though Pat has been a part of the first two segments of this session, what happens in this round, including the voting is to remain with the individuals sitting here and that includes you, Sonja and Celest. Agreed? (Affirmative nods)

*I rose and put the talking stick in the top hat. Jess, who we hadn't heard from was the first to pick it up.*

**Jess as speaker:** I don't have to repeat what you said, right? (I shook my head no) Okay, good. I haven't said anything yet, but I've been listening. I want to say that I never heard any remorse from Pat. She stated that if she had it to do over again, she would do things differently, but I don't believe she has any idea how close she came to dividing this group when she left and now she is back after we've just healed and she's doing it again.

*Jess rose and dropped the stick in the hat and April picked it up.*

**April as designated listener:** What I understood you to say, Jess, is that you don't believe Pat cares that she almost caused the group to fold back in May; if she had the chance to do things differently, yadda, yadda. Correct?

**Jess as speaker:** I guess so.

**Paula on clarification:** Phyllis, that's not what I understood Jess to say.

**Phyllis as leader:** Okay, Paula. What is your understanding?

**Paula on clarification:** I understood Jess to say that Pat didn't have any remorse. To me remorse means feeling guilty, having regrets. I don't know whether Pat even knows to what extent her actions affected the group. I know I didn't tell her. April's version, in my opinion, sounds like she believes Pat doesn't have any feelings for the group at all. I don't think that's true.

**Jess as speaker:** Paula comes closer to what I meant. I said I don't know if Pat knew the chaos she caused. I'm just angry that all of us are back in this spot again.

**Phyllis as leader:** Are you finished, Jess? (Jess nods yes) April, you are still the official designated listener. Will you take another stab at it?

**April as designated listener:** Sure. I'm glad you stepped in, Paula. Jess, what I understand you to have said now is that you don't know if Pat is sorry for the trouble she caused, and we don't even know if she is aware of it. You said, and we all heard Pat say that if she had it to do over she might do things differently, and you said you are upset that we are going through this again. Is that accurate, Jess? (Jess nods)

**April as speaker:** Well, this is a fantastic process. When I stood up to be Jess' designated listener, I was pretty angry, and I see things differently now. I haven't changed my mind about what I wanted to say though. I believe that everyone deserves second chances. I do believe Pat cares about this group. She's been a member for about the same length of time that I have, which is ten years. I would like to have her back in the group.

*April places the stick in the hat, and Amy picks it up.*

**Amy as designated listener:** What I understood you to say April is that you appreciate the Talking Stick process and see its value. It helped you understand Jess' view, but it did not change your perspective. You would like to give Pat a second chance and ask her to come back because you feel she has shown she does care about the group through her long-standing membership. Good? (April: that was perfect.)

**Amy as speaker:** I want to say that during my lifetime I've done a lot of things that I'm not proud of; some were spontaneous, some got a lot of consideration. They felt right at the time, but there is always hindsight. I dated a married man for several months when I was in my twenties. He instigated it, and I thought I was madly in love. It was not only dumb but very hurtful to his wife and family and over the years, I've had many regrets. I'm not saying that is the situation between Pat, Greg, Chris, whatever. I'm not ready to judge anyone for something that I have done, and I feel Pat should have a second chance just like April.

*Amy places the stick, and Nadene picks it up.*

**Nadene as designated listener:** Amy, what I understood you to say is you've done things in your life that you regret, such as dating a married man. You are aware that the only situation you know anything about is your own and don't know anything about what happened between Pat, Greg, and Chris. You have regrets about your relationship and how it affected his family. You feel that Pat should have a second chance. I may be reading something into this, but I think that is supposed to be part of the "understanding" process, but I believe you think you were judged back when you had your relationship, and you feel that some of us will judge Pat in making our decision today. Am I right? (Amy slowly nods yes)

**Nadene as speaker:** I know that Phyllis is the leader and is giving direction, but as a participant, I hope we do not continue bearing our souls and sharing events that happened twenty-five years ago for which we have regrets. Sorry, if that sounds harsh, Amy, but I feel we all need to stay in the present. What I heard today that resonated with me was when Pat said she left because she thought it would be too awkward for her to be part of the group since Chris was a member now. I know she tried to retract it, but feel her original words are her true feelings. She has a selfish streak, and I've always loved her for who she is, but it is there. Even if Chris is gone, if Pat comes back there will be chaos for a long time. I feel it will put a damper on the group and the charity and social functions we carefully planned for this coming year, and I hate to see that happen.

*Nadene puts the stick in the top hat, and Tracy advances.*

**Tracy as designated listener:** What I understood you to say, Nadene, is that a Talking Stick should be objective and not the place to be projecting our regrets or insecurities onto another or the group. In fact, we should never do that, not just in a Talking Stick. We need to stay in the present to understand what is said. I believe you feel Pat left the group because she was worried about her feelings of awkwardness, and it wasn't until today when it came up that she considered everyone else and then tried to restate her feelings. You feel that if Pat comes back there is going to be a lot of awkwardness for a long time and it will affect the whole group. Nadene? (Nadene nods)

*Tracy, Susan, Paula, Cindy, and Janice all pitched with comments similar to what had been said. Tanya and I passed on our right to speak.*

**Phyllis as leader:** Everyone has had a chance to pitch in this Conflict Resolution round. What remains is taking a vote.

The officers decided that Pat must have a two-thirds majority to be reinstated. We have fifteen members, fourteen actually, if we remove Chris based on her letter. Celest, Sonja, and Josie have agreed to go along with the majority vote of the group, so there are eleven of us on the wheel today. We will need eight "yes" votes to reinstate Pat.

The voting round will use circular and not the popcorn style, and there will be no Guarantee step. I will start and pass to Susan. Sonja are you ready to record votes? (Sonja nods)

Phyllis votes: I vote "no." Phyllis passes the stick to Susan.
Susan votes: I vote "no." Susan passes the stick to Jess.
Jess votes: I vote "no." Jess passes to Paula.
Paula votes: I vote "no." Paula passes to Nadene.
Nadene votes: I vote "no." Nadene passes to Cindy.
Cindy votes: I vote "no." Cindy passes to Tanya.
Tanya votes: I vote "no." Tanya passes to April.
April votes: I vote "yes." April passes to Amy.
Amy votes: I vote "yes." Amy passes to Janice.
Janice votes: I vote "no." Janice passes to Tracy.
Tracy votes: I vote "no." Tracy passes to Phyllis.

**Phyllis as leader:** Sonja will you give us the votes?

**Sonja as recorder:** There are nine "no" votes and two "yes" votes. There isn't a two-thirds majority.

**Phyllis as leader:** We achieved our desired result for this Conflict Resolution. We have a consensus, and that is what we set out to accomplish. We will not reinstate Pat.

Let's take a five-minute break. If you don't have to leave the space, I'd appreciate you staying. I'm going outside to ask Pat to come back in, and we will get the last of our four-part session going.

I will be announcing our decision, and then everyone will have one last chance to comment on the outcome or the Talking Stick session in general. Let me remind everyone that how you or anyone else voted is not to be talked about with anyone other than the individuals that are sitting here right now.

## Difficult Discussion Session

**Phyllis as leader:** At this time, I change our purpose to a Difficult Discussion session and welcome you back, Pat.

As you and I discussed before, Pat, the officers decided that there needed to be a two-thirds majority vote for reinstatement. We did not reach that majority.

It was a difficult decision for many of us, and we are going to have one more round so anyone who chooses can reflect on the decision or the process. There is no Guarantee step in a reflection round. Anyone who wishes can pick up the stick and begin.

*Nadene picked up the stick.*

**Nadene as speaker:** Pat, you and I go way back, and I believe you know how much I care for you. As president, I will say that the circumstances of your leaving strongly affected the group and it has just been the last couple of months that there was some semblance of normalcy. I'm not sure we could withstand more turmoil and still function. No one can talk about how they or anyone else voted, and I don't believe I am violating that promise now. One of the Rules of Engagement that Phyllis read initially concerned never engaging in a Talking Stick unless you do so for the good of the whole group. I feel that influenced votes and individuals were not voting against you personally.

*Nadene replaced the stick, and Amy was next.*

**Amy as speaker:** Pat, you mentioned in your opening remarks that you wanted to renew old friendships. It reminded me that I've had a lot going on and haven't been the friend to you that I should have. I feel sorry about that. I too want to get our friendship going again. Let's put something on the calendar before we all leave today.

*Amy put the talking stick in the top hat, and Pat picked up.*

**Candidate Pat as speaker:** I want to thank all of you for committing so much of your Saturday afternoon to do this. I certainly have a new perspective on how many of you saw my behavior when I left, and I can easily see why you felt the way you did, although I can tell you that for the most part, my intentions were completely different than you think. Just like Chris, I care very much about the group and would not want a split to be on my shoulders, so I believe you made the right choice today. I do hope that we all continue our friendships in whatever way you feel appropriate. I am still right here in town too. Thank you.

*Without looking around Pat put the stick in the top hat and then took her seat and after a moment, Susan moved to get the stick.*

**Susan as speaker:** This was my first Talking Stick, and I arrived with my mind made up as to what I was going to do. It was fascinating the way the talking stick brought out the sincerity in everyone. Some of you were angry, and some were sad, but everyone spoke from their heart. I went back and forth on my decision but believe that because of the Talking Stick experience I made the right choice. I'm happy I participated. Thank you all.

*Susan nodded to everyone and then placed the stick in the hat. Paula picked it up.*

**Paula as speaker:** It was my first Talking Stick too. I had no idea what to expect, but now that I have experienced one I would like to learn how to conduct one. We sure could have used this last year during school board meetings. We might have gotten John Davis to shut up. Also, I think my grandkids need this. Do you do this with kids, Phyllis?

*Paula walked to the center with the stick, and I took it from her.*

**Phyllis as speaker:** I want to thank the officers and all of you for trusting me as your leader. I believe in the process and yes to both of your comments, Paula. I know John Davis and would love to see him under a Talking Stick's Rules of Engagement. LOL I'm holding workshops beginning next month on how to become a certified Coach and Talking Stick Facilitator. If anyone is interested, let me know. Your second question about kids is that I have worked with kids as young as five and they love it.

*I walked back to the center and placed the stick. Everyone ended up commenting.*

**Phyllis as leader:** We achieved our desired result for this Difficult Discussion. We have all had a chance for one last reflection.

There is three Completion Status' for Talking Sticks: Successful, Stalemate, and Agreeing to Disagree. This session was a Success. Keep in mind that a Success does not necessarily mean leaving elated or jubilant. You may leave a little disappointed with the outcome, but you should feel that the process was fair and just. Hopefully, you see another's view that you didn't before. Although it may be different from your own, you now see it as valid and appreciate the other person's frame of reference having walked in their shoes.

I want to thank everyone who participated, including you, Sonja and Celest. We haven't heard a lot from you and want you to know you are very much appreciated. Thanks, Nadene for arranging the space with the school board.

I close this Talking Stick.

# Chapter 5
# Types of Talking Sticks

Welcoming
Brainstorming
Fact Finding
Difficult Discussions
Conflict Resolution
Q&A

## *What Type of Talking Stick Do You Need?*

Are you looking for new ideas? You may want a Brainstorming or Fact Finding session. Do you want to jump-start an off-site corporate board of directors meeting? A Welcoming process is what you should start with, and there are numerous options. Maybe you need a consensus on how a group is divided or a final decision on a project. A Fact Finding session seems logical, but with more scrutiny, you might decide on a Difficult Discussion. Is there a conflict between two or more people that isn't resolving itself and requires an intervention? That sounds like a Conflict Resolution but getting everyone on a level playing field to decide may necessitate a Fact Finding, and you might discover it's only a Difficult Discussion.

This chapter and Chapter 6 – Planning Your Session should answer your questions and help you decide not only what type of Talking Stick you need, but how to make it practical and efficient, or zany and memorable. We've got planning down to a science.

## *Personal-Family Talking Sticks*

You'll note that Personal-Family isn't a type mentioned in the list above. It's not a type, but a category. It's separated from business for only one reason, and that is intimacy. Intimate discussions deserve special considerations.

Utilizing Talking Stick sessions for personal and family matters is the most common of all uses and talking sticks have replaced those *other sticks* that in the past received so much use in many households.

The Personal-Family format (format means seating arrangement), is so simple that I neglect it and go into considerably more detail explaining the more complex forms and styles (flow of the dialog) used by clubs, businesses, corporations, and even town councils. At first glance, someone only interested in a simple, fast solution might believe a Talking Stick too complicated for their needs. I guarantee it is not, and, both families, and businesses have similar challenges.

I discuss Formats and Styles in detail in Chapter 6 – Planning Your Session.

| | Challenges | |
|---|---|---|
| Type | Personal-Family | Business or Others |
| Welcoming Sessions | Infrequent family reunions – kids feel grown up when they are recognized | Networking socials – out of town VIPs – sales meetings – board meetings |
| Brainstorming Sessions | Determining family events – the best way to divide chores – decide to get a piano or take music lessons – | Decide on the next fundraising project – possible features of a new product – ideas to enhance customer |

|  | incentives to improve grades | support – new digital marketing ideas |
|---|---|---|
| Fact Finding Sessions | What happened when teens were joyriding – circumstances surrounding fight at school | Research on the best source for components – how employees feel about working from home |
| Difficult Discussions | Change in jobs means chores neglected – need a solution to kids tattling on each other | Employee warnings for job performance – clear tension between employees |
| Conflict Resolution Sessions | Need a solution for lack of college funds – child custody situation needs resolving | Resolve arguments to get a required majority vote – determine if harassment case is going to court |

## Preparation is Paramount

Personal-Family Talking Sticks can use any of the six types, but the intimacy of the participants may cause the sessions to be more emotional. A joke among facilitators is that it's standard procedure to bring a box of tissues to every process.

A family can prepare by regularly scheduling light-hearted sessions, so everyone is familiar with the protocol. It can make it easier when more severe processes are needed.

Also, remember that dealing with emotional issues may feel more demanding. In many Personal-Family sessions, there are just two people, which means continuously switching back and forth from being the speaker to the designated listener with no breaks. Both individuals have to be "on" the whole time. It requires dedicated focus and commitment. Don't agree to this type of Talking Stick after working long hours or when you are exhausted for other reasons.

See Chapter 3 – Dad and the "D" Grade
See Chapter 8 – /Personal-Family Session Stories/The Youngest Talking Stick Facilitator
See Chapter 6 – /Use a Barometer Indicator to Gauge Progress

See Chapter 8 – /Personal-Family Session Stories/Best Friends, Nancy and Sue

## *Start at An Early Age*

Before moving on to the types, I want to say that your kids are probably not too young to start learning the process. One can find one of my favorite stories, which I titled *The Youngest Talking Stick Facilitator* in Chapter 8 – Stories and Examples. Dirk was five-years-old when he facilitated his first Talking Stick.

Kids are naturals with the process, and when I've taught classes, they generally find additional topics to discuss so they can keep going never wanting to quit.

Their favorite rule is what I call the *equality rule*; Rule 4 of the Rules of Engagement states: All participants are equal. They pick up on this right away and realize that whether it's with their teachers, parents, or other kids, the playing field is level. They love the respect they are given and proud to give it back.

There are a couple of issues that challenge some of the younger kids initially though, and they are:

- *Everyone has the right to their own opinion,* and
- *All opinions are valid.*

If they've been fighting with their little brother or another kid at school, they do not want to believe there are two sides to the story, and that both could be correct. For many, it is the first time they get to *walk in another person's shoes*, and it is very enlightening for them.

## *Welcoming Sessions*

**Get Creative**

Welcoming sessions are for creating great beginnings, introducing folks, helping individuals get to know each other comfortably, and well, welcoming. Because the events are typically simple, the Guarantee can be fun and educational. Get creative. It can help everyone remember names better, and if participants are new to the process, it gives them an informal time to learn the protocol for passing the talking stick and mastering the art of repeating what they understood the speaker to say.

The Guarantee may be skipped to save time or because other types of Talking Stick sessions will follow, and these are called Simple Welcomings.

See Appendix F – Simple Talking Stick Structure

**Guidance for Participants**

Many times, Welcoming sessions are a one-step process of passing the talking stick with everyone stating their name. Even though they are elementary for those who are familiar with a particular crowd of people or who have participated in Talking Sticks before, they can be intimidating for someone who has no idea what to expect. Instead of the process helping them to feel comfortable and accepted it might do the opposite and cause tension.

The leader or facilitator may be able to alleviate this by giving specific instructions. Individuals generally feel comfortable talking about themselves, so the leader might ask them to recall a favorite story that correlates with the event. Later during the function, the story may act as a conversation starter for others who might be a little shy and hesitate in approaching someone new.

When given guidance, it can help participants focus their thoughts and find a purpose. And, for individuals who consider the events just routine, it's nice to change things up. I tell a story about a Sisterhood group that I belonged to in Chapter 8, and there are numerous other examples throughout the book.

See Chapter 5 – /Welcoming Session
See Chapter 8 – /Welcoming Sessions/A Sisterhood Welcoming Session
See Chapter 8 – /Welcoming Sessions/Break the Ice or Get Down to Business?
See Chapter 8 – /Welcoming Sessions/Who Moved the Chocolate?

## *Brainstorming and Fact Finding Sessions*

### The Difference Between Brainstorming and Fact Finding

At times there seems little difference between Brainstorming and Fact Finding sessions. For the most part, the difference is the purpose and desired results.

1. With Brainstorming the purpose is generally to be as creative as possible, conceptualizing, conceiving, and generating as many ideas as possible for later consideration. No idea is too farfetched or absurd. They are fast-paced, wild and crazy discussions. A leader or facilitator doesn't need to provide a lot of guidance unless they get entirely out of control.

Popcorn style works exceptionally well with the lively and spontaneous nature of this type of session. No one wants to inhibit the enthusiasm or wait their turn if they are 180 degrees on the other side of the wheel from the current speaker. One consideration of a leader or facilitator should be to ensure everyone has a chance to share their ideas and make sure one person or group doesn't monopolize the time.

2. With a Fact Finding the purpose is to uncover the current pertinent information regarding a subject and many times the desired result is to discuss what is found during the session to enable digging deeper. Typically, no one is looking for farfetched ideas. As the name states, with a Fact Finding, they are looking for facts. These sessions are generally slower-paced, deliberate, and concern more detailed issues. With all that said, many times the results are similar to Brainstorming.

   Popcorn or circle style will work equally well with a Fact Finding.

Consider recording for both types to ensure nothing important gets missed.

Here are some examples of Brainstorming sessions:

See Chapter 8 – /Brainstorming Sessions/Brainstorming for the Holidays
See Chapter 8 – /Brainstorming Sessions/Wheel of Fortune FABs

Examples of Fact Finding sessions:

See Chapter 8 – /Fact Finding Sessions/The Home-court Advantage
See Chapter 8 – /Fact Finding Sessions/Just Getting the Facts
See Chapter 8 – /Conflict Resolution Sessions/The Trade Show Conflict Story

Other examples of interest:

See Chapter 3 – Dad and the "D" Grade
See Chapter 4 – /Win-Win or Lose-Lose

See Chapter 6 – /Formats and Styles – Opening, Rotation, Closing

## *Difficult Discussions*

I believe Talking Stick sessions originated because there are so many types of difficult discussions and so many people avoiding them. When everyone learned they could promote respect, boost self-esteem, and get the problematic discussion out of the way by using a simple tool backed by the Rules of Engagement, things changed. And, knowing they were guaranteed to be understood, they found the courage to do what they couldn't do before.

**Courage Found**

I young boy told me in confidence that his parents needed to know about the bullying he received at school, but he was reluctant to say anything. He said his father was big on we don't air our dirty laundry in public. I couldn't see how being bullied was dirty laundry, but somehow the boy did. He wanted to know if using a talking stick would make it easier to talk to his dad. I said I thought so, but he would be the one to decide. I showed him how to pass with proper protocol, and once he held the stick he closed his eyes, and a huge smile spread across his face. "Yeah," he said, "it works."

See Chapter 8 – /Difficult Discussions/Two Sets of Rules
See Chapter 8 – /Difficult Discussions/Amy's Eating Disorder
See Chapter 8 – /Difficult Discussions/The Italian Mother-In-Law
See Chapter 8 – /Conflict Resolution Sessions/The Trade Show Conflict Story

**Agreeing to Disagree**

Agreeing to Disagree as "status," along with the other two terms used to indicate how a session ends, is discussed in Chapter 6 – /Ending a Session When the Barometer Indicates. Agreeing to Disagree is used when the desired outcome is not met, but there is still hope. It may carry a twinge of disappointment, but the fact that the parties showed up and completed a session, and there's a good chance because of their experience they will come back to the table in the future.

**Intending to Disagree**

Agreeing to Disagree is also a tactic used on occasion in Difficult Discussions to help participants believe the session has no hidden agenda or duplicitous motive.

The first time I heard of this tactic, the wise facilitator blatantly told the participants upfront that he knew there would never be a meeting of the minds; agreement was not expected. Erin's and Nico's parents caused the young couple so much pain during their first years of marriage they were willing to do anything to try and ease the situation. The conflict stemmed from religious backgrounds, and past experiences always ended in shouting matches with both groups feeling disrespected. Nico hoped this time the parents would not only leave with a better understanding of the other's religious beliefs but an appreciation of their beauty and similarities.

The knowledge that Nico and Erin intended for them to agree to disagree automatically relieved them of all pressure and they began the experience much more open-minded and relaxed.

See Chapter 8 – /Difficult Discussions/Nicos and Erin

## *Conflict Resolution*

### Lawsuit or Litigation vs. Mediation

It's not pretty, but it is a fact, we live in a world where many people don't think twice before suing someone. Almost every contract today has a clause that makes signers agree to mediation before running off to court if there is a dispute. Although the Talking Stick process is rarely included in contracts, it has contributed to settling thousands of conflicts out of court.

It should be the first line of defense when there is conflict. If the Rules of Engagement are precisely followed, and the sessions carried out professionally, individuals and businesses will take it seriously.

**Facilitators Should Be Mandatory**

I discuss the difference between a leader of a Talking Stick and a facilitator in Chapter 6 – /Leaders and Facilitators. Briefly, a leader is a party in a Talking Stick that agrees to additional duties. A facilitator is always a third party and completely impartial. In certain situations, a facilitator may be called in to help a participant feel more confident or safer. For Conflict Resolution Talking Sticks I think it should be mandatory for safety sake.

In Chapter 8 there is a story about Joyce and Don and a child custody case. The reference is below. It's not part of the story, but I found out after the fact that Joyce was not completely honest with me when she called and asked if I could come to California and facilitate her session. I hadn't seen Don for six months and didn't realize the extent of their estrangement. She confessed months later that she'd gotten to the point of being petrified of him but hadn't wanted to tell me. You can see in the story that everything turns out fine, but it might not have if she hadn't found a facilitator.

See Chapter 4 – /Talking Stick/Conflict Resolution
See Chapter 8 – /Personal-Family Sessions/The Youngest Talking Stick Facilitator
See Chapter 8 – /Conflict Resolution Sessions/Joyce and Don Child Custody Session
See Chapter 8 – /Conflict Resolution Sessions/Town Council Mediation in Colorado
See Chapter 8 – /Conflict Resolution Sessions/The Fifteen-step Action Plan
See Chapter 8 – /Conflict Resolution Sessions/The Trade Show Conflict Story

# Chapter 6
# Planning Your Session

Although attire, rituals, and traditions of ceremonies have diverged, the structure of celebrations has changed little for hundreds, if not thousands of years.

Psychologists say that when there is an ordered progression to an event, it is more memorable for the participants; they will also be more relaxed and receptive.

Depending on the type of Talking Stick you choose, you may use most of the points in this chapter or only a few. This chapter covers:

- guidelines,
- formats and styles,
- options to create unique and memorable events, and
- insight on preparation for unanticipated situations.

## *Is a Talking Stick Session Appropriate for Your Topic or Group?*

Before jumping into a Talking Stick, there are certain things to consider.

Talking Sticks work for five-year-olds to one-hundred-five-year-olds; from the kitchen to the conference room, which covers most territory, but nothing works 100% of the time.

Here are two vital issues to think about while planning.

1. Rule 2 of the Rules of Engagement is: The environment of a Talking Stick should always be one of respect.

   Ask yourself if the parties are willing and capable of coming together with an attitude of respect. Are they ready? Are issues too painful to discuss right now? Does someone have a mental challenge that would prevent them from following a protocol?

2. Rule 8 states: Where a resolution is required, all participants should agree to resolve the issue for the highest good of all parties.

   Is there a consensus to find a resolution? Does one person want an answer, but you doubt others?

Just as individuals need to speak for themselves, hopefully, they will participate in a Talking Stick because they desire to find solutions and not because they want to please another or for some other reason not their own. If there is an underlying unresolved issue, this may not be a time to plan a Talking Stick or consider tackling the unresolved issue before the current one. Without doing this, it could be like putting a band-aid on the symptom without seeking the cause of the problem.

Here are a couple of examples:

See Chapter 4 – /Fact Finding/Janice as Speaker
See Chapter 4 – /Fact Finding/Cindy as Designated Listener

## Who's Who in a Talking Stick?

You wouldn't have a Talking Stick session unless someone had something they wanted to say and felt strongly about being understood. They are the speaker and could end up being the leader, or just a participant in a session. There may only be two participants, or there could be twenty or more, and thus two or twenty plus speakers. In one type of Talking Stick called a Q&A, a participant called a candidate will also be a speaker.

In some situations, a facilitator is brought in to run the session when a third-party or someone completely impartial is needed.

A Talking Stick may require a recorder to act as a registrar, public official, clerk, or just someone to make sure details don't get missed. A timer is frequently used to keep a group moving and ensure everyone receives equal time to pitch their opinions. Recorders and Timers are generally not active participants in the session.

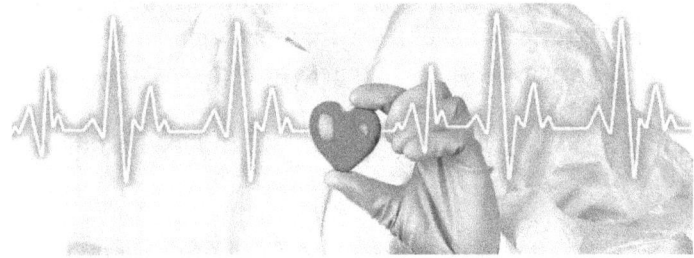

**Designated Listener**

The person with the most significant duty of the whole session is the participant acting as the designated listener because they are responsible for accomplishing the Guarantee. They repeat what they heard and understood the speaker to say to the speaker's satisfaction. They are the Heart of the Talking Stick.

See Chapter 6 – /Leaders and Facilitators
See Chapter 6 – /Timer and Recorder
See Chapter 7 – Speaker and Listener Tips and Etiquette

## *Purpose, Desired Result, Barometer Indicator, Completion Status*

It's quite common to begin the planning process by trying to decide what type of Talking Stick you should use when it might be easier to determine the purpose, desired result, barometer indicator, or even the completion status first. After making those decisions, the type of session may be apparent. To start, here are some definitions.

**The Purpose**

Begin by asking: What is the purpose? Why do I want to have this Talking Stick?

The purpose is generally the choice of the leader or whoever made the decision to have a session, but an entire group could be party to the decision.

A Welcoming session's purpose is primarily introductions, but the leader or facilitator can make the event much more interesting by enhancing the process with ideas that complement the occasion.

See Chapter 8 – /Welcoming Sessions/A Sisterhood Welcoming Session

Mr. Swanson's reason or purpose for his Talking Stick with his son was brought about by a phone call from one of Derik's teachers and Derik's close-to-failing Chemistry grade. Deciding the type of session in a case like this is simple; Mr. Swanson wanted answers, and a Fact Finding session or Personal/Family session was adequate.

See Chapter 3 – Dad and the "D" Grade

The purpose of the Talking Stick in the story of Splitting the Group is to determine whether to reinstate a past member of a group who left without warning and with even less warning wants to return. This scenario further complicated because the group's knowledge of the situation comes from several sources, including rumors, speculation, conjecture, and a little first-hand experience. To make an informed decision in the group's best interest, the first step should be a consensus of facts before moving on to other choices. The type of Talking Stick necessary for this purpose is not as clear.

See Chapter 4 – Splitting the Group

**Determine the Desired Result**

With unlimited time and funds, you might point blindfolded at a map to find your next vacation destination or go to the airport and jump on the next flight out not caring where it's going. It's an adventure. Most people are more comfortable with planning. And, with a Talking Stick many times there's no second chance, so knowing your destination is imperative.

The desired result doesn't mean having the answer before starting the session. It indicates something on the order of:

- to start the meeting off on a positive note and welcome the new members, or
- hear our son's side of the story without him feeling intimidated, or
- get a resolution to the conflict, or
- find out how our employees feel about working from home instead of the office, or
- allow all parties to voice their opinion, or
- let the members ask the candidate questions, so they understand her policies

As a participant, leader, or facilitator, it's imperative to foresee the destination; know the purpose and desired result.

See Chapter 4 – /The Talking Stick

**Use a Barometer Indicator to Gauge Progress**

Not knowing where you are in the process can be just as detrimental as not knowing the destination. If planners set the barometer indicator, so everyone has three chances to speak, it's easy to track when the session is complete. But, if there's no agreed upon number and the desired result is to allow everyone to state their opinion, it will be much harder to keep the process on track and know when it is nearing completion.

Barometer indicators vary based on the type of Talking Stick. Here are some examples:

- we want to brainstorm at least 50 new ideas, or
- we will pass the stick until all speakers are complete (complete indicates that everyone passes on their right to speak – example below), or
- we will continue until we get a two-thirds majority, or the talking stick has gone around four times, or
- if we don't get a unanimous vote after three rounds, we will end the session with a Stalemate.

See Chapter 6 – /Passing on Your Right to Speak
See Chapter 6 – /Ending a Session When the Barometer Indicates

**Poor Intentions, No Desired Result, No Barometer**

Without much planning a couple decided to have a Personal-Family Talking Stick to *air grievances* over hurt feelings; both have recently had affairs. An hour into the session they are still at each other's throats, and it's becoming more heated. The process should be complete, and there's no reason to prolong the agony, but because there was no barometer indicator to gauge progress this session could go on for days, with each digging a deeper hole for themselves.

Planning to do the session in two parts or to use a facilitator may have brought different results. These would be the logical segments:

- Initially a Difficult Discussion with the desired outcome of allowing time to air grievances but have a barometer indicator cap it with a specific amount of time or a certain number of times each can speak.

- Second a Fact Finding or Conflict Resolution with the purpose of finding a way to forgive each other and move on. This segment should also have an indicator to show if the forgiveness part was progressing, imminent, or should terminate as a Stalemate.

See Chapter 6 – /Leaders and Facilitators

**Not Knowing When to Shut Up**

During workshops, I teach on sales I lecture on the *perils of not knowing when to shut up*. Most of the students find this very humorous until I explain, and then they realize they have probably done it.

Salespeople spend an inordinate amount of time in training on their products or services. They watch videos, read, memorize facts, and go to seminars led by sales gurus until they pop out of their skins. When they come face to face with potential clients, they spew this information all over them. Some clients immediately run for the hills, but a few get hooked. But then there's a problem. The salespeople are so excited about their entire spiel; they aren't willing to let a client sign until they have the complete performance. They didn't shut up when they should. They did not have a barometer indicator to gauge the progress of their sale. By the end of the pitch, the bored client is turned off and walks away.

The same thing frequently happens in Talking Stick sessions if barometer indicators get missed.

See Chapter 6 – /Personal or Family Talking Sticks/Poor Intentions, No Desired Result, No Barometer

**Completion Status**

There are three ending statuses:

- Successful
- Stalemate
- Agreeing to Disagree

See Chapter 6 – /Ending a Session When the Barometer Indicates

## *Merging Types of Talking Sticks*

By this time in your planning, you may know which type of Talking Stick you need. If there is still some question, the reason may be because a sequence of functions is necessary to solve your challenge, like the example in Chapter 4 – Splitting the Group.

See Chapter 8 – /Conflict Resolution Stories/The Trade Show Conflict Story

List the steps to achieve your desired result, consider each function—Brainstorming, Difficult Discussion, Fact Finding—as a separate segment of the Talking Stick session. I don't recommend changing purposes, desired outcome, or types of Talking Sticks without explicitly closing one and beginning another.

Logically a Brainstorming Talking Stick could progress into a Fact Finding or Conflict Resolution process, but I suggest closing out the Brainstorming session, taking a quick break, stating the new purpose and desired result and beginning anew.

These extra steps may seem cumbersome and unnecessary, but I believe the examples will help you see the reasoning for this. When opening the new process, make sure all relevant decisions from the previous session are on the table, so there's no confusion.

See Chapter 6 – /Personal or Family Talking Sticks/Poor Intentions, No Desired Result, No Barometer

## *NO Punishment NO Discipline*

The desired result will never include punishment. Rule 9 of the Rules of Engagement states: Participants never receive discipline as a direct result of something that is said or revealed during a Talking Stick.

Who would come clean, be perfectly honest, admit to something they didn't have to if they knew they were subject to immediate disciplinary action? Without the commonly called *NO Punishment NO Discipline Rule*, a Talking Stick would never work. A guilty conscious might cause someone to confess, but it would be rare. How many teenagers volunteer that they cheated on a test before they get caught? They would need a reason.

To a degree, the volunteering happens in law enforcement when a criminal *pleads guilty to a lesser charge*. In those cases, there will likely still be punishment involved, but the criminal hopes for a lighter sentence. In a Talking Stick, the discipline is, minimally, deferred, or eliminated if the conduct never happens again.

So, punishment can never happen as a result of a Talking Stick, but it is okay to discuss a type of punishment that could result if a specific behavior or other criteria doesn't change in the future. If this may be a point of discussion, plan for it if possible including the parameters and who is responsible for leading the discussion.

See Chapter 4 – /The Talking Stick Session/Win-Win or Lose-Lose
See Chapter 8 – /Difficult Discussions/Two Sets of Rules
See Chapter 8 – /Difficult Discussions/Amy's Eating Disorder

## *Leaders and Facilitators*

In casual situations, the person requesting the Talking Stick becomes the leader by default. In a Welcoming, the host is generally the leader unless they designate someone else. In any case, the leader or facilitator will arrange the location, contact all participants, and make all other arrangements. Below are additional requirements for leaders and facilitators.

**Definition of a Leader**

A leader can be a participating member of a group that is voted or appointed to hold the position. They must be familiar with the Talking Stick Rules of Engagement and believe they can lead without bias. They must be impartial when the session's protocol requires it but may speak their own opinion freely when they hold the talking stick or are the designated listener.

**Definition of a Facilitator**

A Talking Stick facilitator is usually a third party who understands the Rules of Engagement, is entirely impartial, and agrees to organize and preside over the session. They have no attachment to the result of the process and will at no time state their own opinion.
**Additional Leader and Facilitator Duties**

Depending on specific sessions, leaders or facilitators are also responsible for additional tasks, such as opening and closing sessions, directing dialog, ensuring that it stays on track, recognizing when barometer indicators have been reached and helping the group to the next stage.

In certain situations, a facilitator may be called in to help a participant feel more confident or safer.

See Chapter 8 – /Joyce and Don's Child Custody Session.

It is extremely rare, but occasionally a participant might need to be asked to leave a session.

See Chapter 6 – /Removing Someone from a Session

All remaining sections in this chapter are essential for leaders and facilitators to understand.

See Chapter 4 – /Welcoming
See Chapter 4 – /Fact Finding/Janice as speaker
See Chapter 4 – /Fact Finding/Nadene as speaker

**Certified Guarantee You Are Understood Initiative Facilitators and Coaches**

Guarantee You are Understood Facilitators and Coaches are always needed. If you have an interest, check Appendix B for more information.

## *Determine the Location for a Session*

It is a matter of Talking Stick etiquette to allow the person who is asked to participate in a session to choose the meeting place, and they should select a neutral location if possible. In a group situation, the leader or facilitator should decide.

It's essential for all parties or groups, to feel comfortable in the setting selected. No one should think they have the *home-court advantage* or be intimidated by their surroundings.

If the Talking Stick is between a parent and child or teenager, the location is even more significant because of the relationship. The kids will likely be intimidated right from the start. The kitchen or family room may seem the logical location, but the child's or teen's bedroom might be chosen instead to give them a *home-court advantage* intentionally.

Couples may choose to meet in their home but should prepare to maintain privacy and eliminate distractions and interruptions. Babysitters should be considered or taking kids to a neighbor or relative.

The final deciding factor for your location could be the format you choose for your Talking Stick session, which is next.

See Chapter 4 – /The Talking Stick/Win-Win or Lose-Lose
See Chapter 8 – /Personal-Family Sessions/Best Friends, Nancy and Sue
See Chapter 8 – /Fact Finding Sessions/The Home-court Advantage

## *Formats and Styles*
## *Opening, Rotation, Closing*

### Personal or Family Format

If there are only two people involved in a personal or family format, it is a simple back and forth passing of the stick and dialog, but the process could compound if there are children or others involved. With two people involved, the person requesting the session, by default becomes the leader.

See Chapter 6 – /Leaders and Facilitators

If others are involved someone needs to make sure everyone has equal time to speak, and this usually is one of the leader's duties.

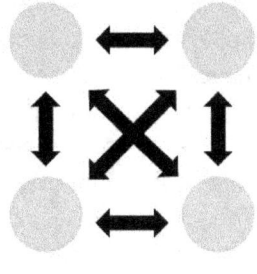

Whether there are two or more participants, the leader opens the session by stating why they initiated the event, and then they begin the dialog. When they have made their *pitch,* (said what they wanted to say) the Guarantee process begins.

See Chapter 6 – /The Guarantee and Proper Passing Protocol

**Personal/Family Format with a Facilitator**

It may be judicious to ask a third-party to be present during a Talking Stick for numerous reasons as was stated above in Leaders and Facilitators. In a Personal/Family session the only difference between a leader and facilitator is the facilitator does not take part in the dialog.

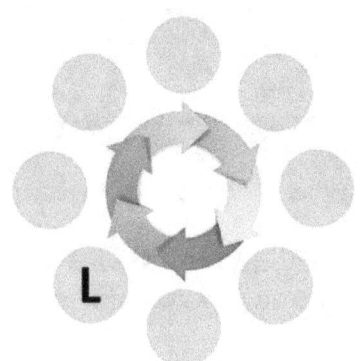

See Chapter 6 – /Leaders and Facilitators
See Chapter 6 – /The Guarantee and Proper Passing Protocol

**Wheel Format with Circle Style with a Leader**

This format and style are the most common and used with all the different types of Talking Sticks. The wheel format means that participants sit in a basic wheel shape. The L in the diagram to the right shows the person in the leadership role.

The circle style means the stick and dialog will move circularly or in a *specified order* every round. This movement contrasts with the popcorn style, which you will see below. Unless defined differently, talking sticks rotate in a clockwise direction.

The leader gives the opening remarks and then becomes the first speaker and starts the dialog by giving their pitch or saying what they have come to share.

The person to their left is their designated listener, and this person begins the Guarantee step. They must repeat what they understood the speaker to say, although everyone on the wheel should be able to do this as well. When the speaker is complete (feels understood), they pass the talking stick to the designated listener, and they become the next speaker. The person to their left becomes the newly appointed listener, and the process continues clockwise.

See Chapter 4 – /The Talking Stick/Welcoming
See Chapter 6 – /Who's Who in a Talking Stick?
See Chapter 6 – /Leaders and Facilitators
See Chapter 6 – /The Guarantee and Proper Passing Protocol

**Wheel Format with Circle Style with a Facilitator**

A gathering with a more formal objective may have a facilitator instead of a leader. As stated before, the facilitator does not take part in the dialog but makes sure the session runs smoothly.

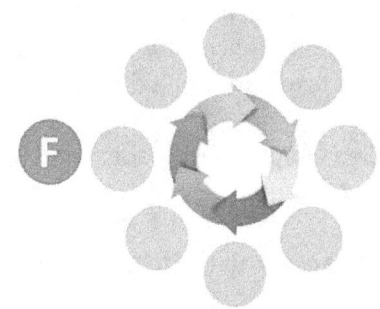

See Chapter 6 – /Leaders and Facilitators

**Wheel Format with Popcorn Style with Leader or Facilitator**

This variation of the wheel format may use either a leader or a facilitator. It is called the popcorn style.

With the popcorn style, the leader or person designated as the facilitator gives the opening remarks. Then either the leader or whoever the facilitator appoints becomes the first speaker and starts the dialog.

When finished, instead of passing the stick to their left for the Guarantee step, they place it in the middle of the wheel, and anyone may choose to step forward and accept it and become the designated listener. As the listener, they face the speaker and go through the same Guarantee step as any designated listener although they are usually holding the stick during the process. When the speaker is *complete* (feels they are understood), the listener becomes the new speaker.

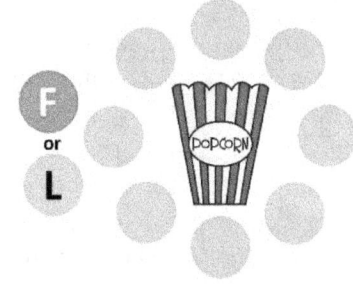

The session is complete when everyone *passes on their right to speak*. At this time, there should be an unfinished Guarantee process, and the leader or the previously designated listener becomes the designated listener to accomplish the current Guarantee.

When using this style, establish rules to ensure that all participants receive the same opportunity to state their views.

See Chapter 6 – /Who's Who in a Talking Stick?
See Chapter 6 – /Leaders and Facilitators
See Chapter 6 – /The Guarantee and Proper Passing Protocol
See Chapter 6 – /Passing on Your Right to Speak

**Theater Format with a Leader or Facilitator**

Theater Format can have either a leader or facilitator and almost always uses the popcorn style because of the seating arrangement of the participants. Large gatherings such as town meetings, or corporate functions favor this format. Generally, only some of the participants choose to speak; the rest are present as spectators.

The rotation is the same as for the wheel format with popcorn style above, and the only significant change is that the leader or facilitator formally recognizes the person that chooses to become the designated listener from the audience. The speaker remains at the podium or front of the room with the talking stick until the Guarantee step is complete before formally relinquishing the stick to the new speaker and taking their seat.

See Chapter 6 – /Who's Who in a Talking Stick?
See Chapter 6 – /Leaders and Facilitators
See Chapter 6 – /The Guarantee and Proper Passing Protocol

**Q&A Combo**

The Q&A Combo could be considered a larger version of a personal Talking Stick where one individual is questioning another. Its origin is like a political debate, and it's used in specific situations when:

1. A person (no more than two), needs to be interviewed by a group of individuals, or
2. A group of individuals needs to be questioned by a person (no more than two).

The person doing the questioning, or the interviewee is the *candidate*.

A Q&A Combo can have a leader or facilitator, a wheel or theater format, and use either a circle or popcorn style. The leader or facilitator opens the session.

In example 1, the candidate generally sits on the wheel, but it's not required. After the opening statement, the candidate gives their opening remarks and then passes the stick or places it in the center depending on the style used. The designated listener is responsible for the Guarantee and then becomes the speaker, and this is where the difference in this type of Talking Stick becomes apparent. Since all dialog is between the participants and the candidate, the candidate is now the designated listener, and the new speaker asks their question or makes their comment. When the new speaker finishes (has said what they wanted), the Guarantee process reverts to the candidate.

In example 2, the most common style of rotation is popcorn, so after the opening statement by the leader or facilitator, the candidate gives their opening remarks and immediately asks their first question or comments and then passes the stick. The session appears to be like any process with a popcorn style, but it becomes apparent after the new speaker is complete and the talking stick returns to the candidate and the become the designated listener. Refer to Wheel Format with Popcorn Style for additional instructions.

See Chapter 4 – /The Talking Stick
See Chapter 6 – /Who's Who in a Talking Stick?
See Chapter 6 – /Leaders and Facilitators

## *The Guarantee and Proper Passing Protocol*

### The Speaker is Finished

We say the speaker is *finished* (compared to *complete* – see The Speaker is Complete below) when they've made their remarks, and they are ready for the Guarantee step.

### The Designated Listener

It is the designated listener's task to *accomplish the Guarantee*. In the Who's Who in A Talking Stick section, I said the designated listener has the most significant duty in a Talking Stick. The Guarantee is the heart of the process.

It is a time when an eruption can send all good intentions out the window. It's vital to remember the speaker may be nervous because of the subject matter or because this is a new experience for them. The designated listener may be anxious because they are uncertain of what they need to do, or they may be hurt or angry over what the speaker has just said. These can be deal breakers.

### Deal Breaker – Deal Maker

Even though Proper Passing Protocol is discussed at length next, remember that the Guarantee process begins with the speaker passing the talking stick to the designated listener. The final step of the passing process is called the eye-lock, and it is a moment when speaker and listener pause and look into each other's eyes. Remaining calm or breathing deep and finding calm in stressful situations and accomplishing this last step with complete respect for the other person can be the deal maker.

Once in a while, someone will complain that the Guarantee step is overcomplicated because the listener must repeat every time. It may seem so, but the extra minute to take a deep breath and relax before repeating something controversial may save the session. Use the reference below for tips on how to make this process go smoothly.

### The Simplest Form

In its purest form, the process is the designated listener must repeat what they understood the speaker to say to the speaker's satisfaction. If the speaker does not feel understood, they have the right to restate their position and ask the listener to repeat once again. The process continues until the speaker feels understood.

## The Extra Mile

In the Rules of Engagement, Rule 8 states: Where a resolution is required, all participants should agree to resolve the issue for the highest good of all parties. When a conscientious listener truly wants to find a solution that is in the best interest of all parties, they go above and beyond. Repeating back what the speaker said is a huge step in communication but to repair damaged relationships the process may need to go deeper. The designated listener should seek to discover the speaker's perspective. To find the meaning behind the words to be able to relate.

See Chapter 4 – /Talking Stick/Cindy as a designated listener
See Chapter 7 – /Designated Listener

## The Speaker is Complete

When they feel understood, we say they are complete, and the designated listener becomes the new speaker after completing the passing protocol.

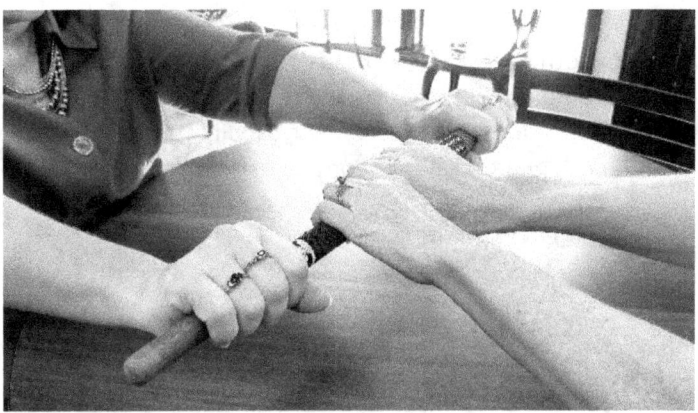

## Proper Passing Protocol

**When passing the talking stick, hold it with both hands close to the ends and present it to the other person. Wait for them to grasp the middle using both of their hands. Make eye contact and hold it for a second, nod slightly and when they have responded release the stick to them.**

### The Gift of Respect

The eye contact or an eye-lock is essential during passing. Many indigenous people say the eyes are the window to the soul. When looking into someone's eyes, the give the *gift of respect* to the other person. In the Rules of Engagement, Rule 2 states: The environment of a Talking Stick should always be one of respect. An eye-lock is the ultimate demonstration of respect during a Talking Stick session.

When working with kids between the ages of 9-11, there's lots of giggling when the boys and girls lock eyes, and I find it quite humorous and enjoy their discomfort. In just a few years they will be seeking reasons to gaze into each other's eyes.

See Chapter 3 – Dad and the "D" Grade
See Chapter 4 – /The Talking Stick/Welcome

### Differences in Formats

In the personal/family and some wheel formats, the speaker generally finishes their pitch and indicates such to the designated listener with a nod or in some other fashion but holds onto the stick until the Guarantee is complete before formally relinquishing the stick. It is the same in theater format with the speaker usually still in the front of the room and the designated listener coming from the audience.

See Chapter 3 – Dad and the "D" Grade
See Chapter 4 – /Talking Stick/Welcome

In a wheel format or Q&A Combo format with a popcorn style, the speaker who is finished places the stick in the middle of the wheel, and someone comes forward to become the designated listener. In this case, the listener holds the stick during the Guarantee step and already has it when the speaker and Guarantee step are complete. So, it is essential for the previous speaker and new speaker to remember to complete the final eye-lock to continue the attitude of respect.

See Chapter 4 – /Talking Stick/Fact Finding
See Chapter 4 – /Talking Stick/Conflict Resolution

**Frame of Reference**

In a group, some individuals may hear or understand the speaker differently. If someone disagrees with the designated listener as they repeat the message, but the speaker doesn't object, the individual with the question is entirely in his or her right to ask for further clarification before moving to the next speaker. Others may be confused as well. They should speak up.

See Chapter 4 – /Talking Stick/Paula on clarification

**Omitting the Guarantee**

There are only a few times when you might consider omitting or skipping the Guarantee step in a Talking Stick session. **In all cases, the stick would still be passed using the proper protocol.**

In a **Simple Welcoming**, the leader or facilitator might choose to skip the Guarantee because of time constraints. In that case, participants would merely introduce themselves and may make an additional remark or two and then pass the stick to the person on their left.

Generally, the Guarantee step is skipped in an **Establishing the Collective** segment because, for the most part, it is a preliminary round to the actual business of the session.

There are no expectations for a Guarantee step when the leader or facilitator gives the **opening remarks**, and the same is true for a **voting round**.

See Chapter 4 – /Talking Stick/Conflict Resolution

One other exception is a **reflection round**. Reflection rounds are last passes before a Talking Stick closes. They are effective anytime and especially useful if there is a status of Stalemate or Agreeing to Disagree. A leader or facilitator can ask for the reflection round to discuss possible next steps.

In the story of Splitting the Group told in Chapter 4, the last round is a Difficult Discussion segment with the purpose of informing Pat of the group's decision and then having a reflection round. Typically, a complete Difficult Discussion session would have speakers, listeners, the Guarantee, etc., but in this case, the only rotation is reflection round, so the decision is made to skip the Guarantee. In cases like this, it is the leader or facilitator's choice.

See Chapter 4 – /Talking Stick/Difficult Discussions
See Chapter 6 – /Ending a Session When the Barometer Indicates – Stalemate or Agreeing to Disagree

## *Passing on Your Right to Speak*

Setting the barometer so that a talking stick is passed around a wheel a certain number of times, or to allow speakers a specific number of times to pitch is typical, and it is easy to gauge progress. But before their limit is up some individuals may be complete and choose to *pass on their right to speak*.

Choosing not to pitch can be done at any time, and it doesn't mean the person is giving up their right to talk forever. They may take the stick when it comes around again.

Note: A person is passing on speaking, not on being a designated listener. If a speaker is expecting someone to be their designated listener, that person must complete the job before passing. Someone cannot *pass on being a designated listener* unless it is specified before a speaker begins.

See Chapter 8 – /Conflict Resolution Sessions/Mutiny in Arizona

## *Plan Your Opening*

Whether there are two people for a Talking Stick or fifty, there should be a brief explanation to set the stage. If you desire a wacky, fun brainstorming event, express this in the opening to get everyone in the mood. I've seen costumes and props used. A Karaoke Club in San Francisco told me they did a Welcoming with karaoke, of course. The Guarantee step was the designated listener repeating the same song as the speaker. From what I understand a few people got tipped off ahead of time, and it was hilarious.

If a group must come together for a significant discussion or decision, make the seriousness of the session known beforehand with your opening. The sincerity with which a Talking Stick opens carries it to a favorable resolution.

Some groups begin with prayer or meditation.

If you are opening a second or subsequent segment, make sure to relate the pertinent results from the previous portion even if it has only been a few minutes since it ended. It's vital that all participants begin each section with the same reference point keeping them on a level playing field.

See Chapter 8 – /Personal-Family Sessions/Nancy's Opening at the Park
See Chapter 8 – /Brainstorming Sessions/Brainstorming for the Holidays
See Chapter 8 – /Brainstorming Sessions/Wheel of Fortune FABs

See Chapter 8 – /Conflict Resolution Sessions/Town Council Mediation Introduction

See Chapter 8 – /Conflict Resolution Sessions/Joyce's Opening for the Child Custody Session

## *Begin in a Positive Space*

Chapter 2 – Rules of Engagement, Rule 2 states: The environment of a Talking Stick should always be one of respect. Even if participants have a desire to resolve issues with the best interest of all concerned initially, stuff happens. By the time they arrive memories of past incidents could have resurfaced, future concerns cropped up, or it could have been a hassle getting to the session, all creating negative energy that doesn't need to go into the process.

Depending on the group, a tradition called *smudging* may be appropriate to clear the air. If asked, a group of metaphysical and non-metaphysical individuals about this tradition, the non-metaphysical folks would say it's just a bunch of mumbo-jumbo, while the spiritual tribe would say there is an actual transformation in the surrounding energy. What is true is the *conscious act* of smudging with the intention of removing negative energy does shift the power, and quantum physics proves this. Here are several options if you choose to do it.

Smudging generally refers to the use of white sage either in a tied bundle form or with the dried leaves crushed and placed in a shell or bowl. Light the sage and brush the smoke over participants to cleanse them of the chaotic energy of the outside world. Some traditions will designate a person to smudge individuals as they enter the space. In others, each person smudges him or herself indicating their desire to take responsibility for themselves and the choices made.

If this feels inappropriate for the group, consider using a sage spray, or setting up a diffuser with sage essential oil before individuals arrive. Sage has a delightful aroma.

## *Establishing a Collective*

Another common opening is called *establishing the collective*. A collective can be two people for a Talking Stick, eight Native American elders gathered around a campfire, fifteen people for a corporate board meeting, the city of Los Angeles, the state of New York, the entire United States of America, or all people on the planet; the number of individuals is not significant. A collective is a group that has come together with a common goal.

At first glance, you might think this is a Welcoming session because the format is similar. A talking stick is passed, and everyone states their name to begin a meeting. To the individuals and groups that use this segment though it has a more profound purpose. They hold that this *conscious act* of creating and setting a *group intention* helps achieve a favorable conclusion for the gathering. The process is not a mere introduction or clerical step.

## *Timer and Recorder*

When working with a group, it is a good idea to have a timer that is not a participant. The same goes for a recorder. Everyone already has a responsibility and when trying to do multiple jobs something is going to be missed.

If using a timer, each person has a specified amount of time to speak. There will always be someone who feels shorted no matter how much time they have, but limits force a speaker to present a concise view that has been thought out and keeps them from creating a filibuster, whether intentional or unintentional. It also suggests a desire to be fair right from the beginning.

Timers can establish a pattern for speakers. For example, the time allotted is five minutes total. The speaker has a four-minute increment and then a one-minute period for a summary. The timer enables their device to beep a couple of times after the first four minutes and then resets it for the next segment. When the time is up, the speaker must wrap up in ten seconds or less or be cut off by the facilitator or leader. Rarely is a timer used in a personal Talking Stick, although sometimes it should.

Another consideration is recording the dialog. Documenting a session was mentioned before, so nothing gets missed. Additionally, if you feel there could be legal repercussions, make sure to record. If you choose a recording, all participants need to be informed.

See Chapter 4 – /Win-Win or Lose-Lose
See Chapter 8 – /Conflict Resolution Sessions/The Trade Show Conflict
    Story

## *Multiple Points of Discussion and Notetaking*

If a speaker has multiple points, they may need to break the list down into small groups or deliver them one at a time to make it easier on the designated listener. If the listener spends time trying to remember a long list of items, they are unlikely to catch the relevance or nuances of each point.

As part of the planning, determine if participants can take paper and pen into the session to jot down notes. If everyone agrees, they should be reminded only to write keywords to jog memory later. It is not a time for writing a response to something the speaker has said.

Since individuals can only speak when they have the talking stick, agreed-upon hand signs to signal the speaker that another moment or two is needed is helpful. Blurting out, "Hold on," in a frustrated tone is not favorable.

See Chapter 8 – /Conflict Resolution Sessions/The Fifteen-step Action Plan

## *Removing Someone from a Session*

It is rare but there might be a necessity to remove someone from a session, so it's good to have a contingency plan.

If a participant blatantly refuses to abide by the Rules of Engagement or is disrupting the session to the degree that the meeting cannot continue; the remainder of the collective may vote to remove the participant from the event. A two-thirds majority vote is necessary for removal.

When this becomes a concern, someone needs to get the attention of either the leader or the facilitator and have them bring the matter to a vote.

## *Ending a Session When the Barometer Indicates*

We previously discussed knowing the purpose, determining the desired result, and agreeing on a barometer indicator to gauge the progress of the session.

When the barometer indicates, it is time to move to the next step, which could be ending a segment, taking a break and starting another, or closing a Talking Stick. Always restate the purpose and desired result at the end of a process. If the session is continuing with another segment, consider giving a brief overview of the upcoming one, especially if individuals need to develop their point of view or make other considerations.

**Completion Status**

There are three ending statuses:

- Successful
- Stalemate
- Agreeing to Disagree

**The Desired Result is Achieved – Successful**

If you look back to the beginning of this chapter to the discussion of determining the desired result, you will remember that it could be brainstorming 50 ideas, passing the talking stick four times around, getting a two-thirds majority vote, when all speakers are complete, or many others.

In the story of Splitting the Group, the achievement of the desired result happened four times:

- during the Welcoming when everyone finished saying their name and learned the protocol for passing the talking stick,

- at the end of the Fact Finding when Pat had answered everyone's questions,

- when participants choosing to speak during the Conflict Resolution were complete and the vote counted, and

- lastly during the Difficult Discussion process when Pat learned of the group's decision and everyone took one more opportunity to reflect on the session.

It was a significant success in Talking Stick jargon, but I' betting not all participants were happy with the result, including Pat. Thus, Success describes the status and achievement of the session, but not necessarily the emotion felt by all the participants.

See Chapter 4 – /Talking Stick/Difficult Discussions

A leader or facilitator should be careful before brandishing a status of Successful, although sometimes it's perfect. For sessions when the stakes were tenuous and the achievement successful, the moment deserves appropriate recognition.

An organization that managed homeschooling programs for kids in Colorado ran into multiple roadblocks locating a venue for their graduation ceremony. The facilitator of a Conflict Resolution Talking Stick tackling the last obstacle had foreseen a favorable conclusion, and much to everyone's surprise had queued up the *Pomp and Circumstance* graduation march for the closing. It was perfect.

## The Desired Result is Not Reached – Stalemate or Agreeing to Disagree

When the barometer indicates the desired result isn't obtainable, the leader or facilitator should consider these options:

1. Try redirecting the individuals or group to the agreed-upon desired outcome by taking a break and reconvening later or getting a consensus to reevaluate the desired results and continue at some time in the future.

2. If the session is a Personal-Family, Difficult Discussion or Conflict Resolution session, the type could change (after closing initial segment) to a Fact Finding or Brainstorming session to explore a possible solution not considered initially, and the Talking Stick continued.

3. Ending with a Stalemate status means the desired result was unreachable. Stalemate status requires a unanimous vote if there are only two individuals, a two-thirds majority vote if there are more participants, or can be used by a facilitator if he/she determines the participants are deliberately disregarding the Rules of Engagement.

4. End and close the session Agreeing to Disagree.

I've never had a Talking Stick that I consider a complete failure; I've always felt there was some movement forward even if the parties were not willing to admit to the advancement at the time. There were processes where participants walked out, but many times those who walked out walked back in again later, and I considered those to be huge successes.

Agreeing to Disagree status signifies the parties tried for an agreement, but the desired result was unreachable for some reason. The reason could be that the results need reevaluation because they aren't feasible at this time. Although Statement sounds negative, it is not necessarily so because the participants may be willing to reconvene at a future date under different circumstances.

There is more to be said about agreeing to disagree in general. There is the status, and then there is the *intent*.

See Chapter 5 – /Difficult Decisions

There were times when I reluctantly agreed to facilitate a Talking Stick believing there was no hope but found myself quite surprised. You don't want to get someone's expectations up carelessly and waste everyone's time but giving someone the benefit of the doubt can have surprising results.

See Chapter 8 – /The Italian Mother-in-Law

## *Closing*

Consider a reflection round no matter the outcome. Pass the stick one last time to ask for thoughts and observations. Depending on the status, ask participants if they are interested in pursuing the issue further at some point or under different circumstances.

Close the session with the same tone as the opening. In the Colorado town council session story, the mayor said a few words to begin, so he also spoke at the end thanking participants for their time and effort. If the event opened with a prayer, it would be appropriate to close with one.

Always show appreciation to everyone that came and participated. Also, thank everyone who worked behind the scenes, like folks in a kitchen or your recorder and timer. Many times, these individuals work very hard with no recognition.

See Chapter 6 – /The Guarantee and Proper Passing Protocol/Omitting the Guarantee

## Get Agreement

Whatever you decide during your planning, make sure all parties to the Talking Stick are aware of and in most cases agree to the purpose, desired result, barometer indicator, and other steps before the session begins.

## Open, Truthful, Heart-to-Heart Communication

Talking Sticks work because individuals can express themselves without fear of criticism, judgment or punishment. The environment should always foster open, truthful, heart-to-heart communication.

# Chapter 7
# Speaker and Listener Tips and Etiquette

## *Speaker Tips and Etiquette*

Follow these tips when speaking or as in Talking Stick jargon, when *pitching*.

**Ground Before Beginning**

Begin by taking several deep breaths and grounding using whatever method works for you. One technique is to hold the stick for a moment, or two feeling its energy or put one end on the floor or earth and imagine drawing that energy upward. Many people feel more centered and calmer after connecting with the power of the planet.

**Make an Eye Connection**

In personal Talking Sticks with just one other person, make direct eye contact before starting. On a wheel of several individuals, it may be more difficult. Be genuine and don't take it to the extreme or let it become theatrical. If the audience is large, it's probably not possible to make eye contact physically with everyone, but an intention can be set to connect with the collective, and this can work just as well. Remember, it's also important to keep the energy and pace of the session moving.

**Criticism**

Remain calm and speak honestly and truthfully from the heart. The stick serves as an invitation and encouragement to talk from the most undefended place inside of one's self. Rule 3 of the Rules of Engagement states: Whatever needs to be said can be without worry of criticism or judgment. The speaker should have no concern over being interrupted, criticized, or judged, especially if they intend to do the same.

See Chapter 2 – Rule 3 of the Rules of Engagement
See Chapter 8 – Other Stories/The Fidgety Young Woman

**Show Confidence – Read It If You Need To**

Be prepared. Do whatever it takes to find confidence. Plan what you are going to say, if possible. There should be no problem reading something if it helps. Be succinct. When presenting facts, always show you have researched the subject or if personal, that you've considered all aspects.

Repetitious or nervous behavior is an indication that someone is not entirely sure of themselves or their beliefs. Pitch with conviction and be done.

**Trauma – Drama with the Designated Listener**

It's imperative the speaker not become defensive if the designated listener misses or blunders parts of the speaker's message or doesn't get the gist of what is said. Several things could be happening.

- They could be nervous because they aren't familiar with the protocol,
- They may have received too much information at one time,
- They could be messing up on purpose trying to stir up some trouble.

## The Speaker's Best Response – I Guess I Didn't Make Myself Clear

Everyone might as well go home if the speaker's reply is, "Well, as usual, you just don't get it."

If the speaker truly wants to resolve the issue, they may have to bite their tongue and take several deep breaths before they reply.

This reply would be much more productive than the one above, "I believe you understood me on point one and two, but I guess I didn't make myself clear on ..."

The speaker must continue to be sincere with a level intonation. A calm, I guess I didn't make myself clear, is very important and if the speaker sticks to the higher ground and assumes, at least initially, that the miscommunication was unintentional the listener may be a little embarrassed if they were trying for trauma-drama and back down. Even if the speaker knows the act to be intentional, they need to ignore it if there is any chance of a successful conclusion.

Both parties need to stay centered and grounded and keep situations from escalating during a Talking Stick. Everyone has come together peacefully to resolve an issue and hopefully it will happen.

If a facilitator is present, it is his or her job to diffuse any tension before it gets out of hand.

Some Talking Stick issues can be very emotional, and emotions are better left outside. Listener and speaker rules of etiquette recommend staying away from anything that could cause drama. Any outburst may look like an attempt to manipulate, and that could ignite both sides.

**Never Try to Change Another's View Through Manipulation**

The most effective course of action to get someone to change their view is for the speaker to state the argument with confidence along with well-researched reasons why they feel strongly about it. Doing this shows they know their mind; that they are leaders and not stooping to deviousness. Someone who is on the fence is much more likely to follow someone who has respect for others and doesn't try to intimidate or manipulate.

Low self-esteem makes someone feel the need to change others to their point of view. We say they need the herd's validation. They look for validation outside themselves because they do not trust their personal intuition. When they don't get it, they doubt themselves. They are not leaders. Be a leader.

**When the Speaker is Finished**

Keeping a Talking Stick moving is essential. As a speaker finishes, they should be ready to pass to their designated listener immediately.

**Passing the Talking Stick**

When you make eye contact with someone, it is much easier to remember that you both desire a resolution for the common good. And, it is much harder to lie or cheat someone after you have looked them in the eye.

# Designated Listener Tips and Etiquette

**The Designated Listener Accomplishes the Guarantee**

The designated listener has the most essential duty in a Talking Stick; they accomplish the Guarantee. They must repeat what they heard and understood the speaker to say to the speaker's satisfaction.

**Always Start With...**

The listener should always start with, "What I understood you to say was..." and then proceed with what they believe the speaker intended.

In an emotional Talking Stick, this is a time when an eruption can send all good intentions out the window. It's important to remember the person across from you may be nervous because of the subject matter or because this is a new experience for them.

Express the details that were important with empathy and communicate them back to the speaker's satisfaction. When the speaker feels understood, we say the speaker is complete.

**Stay in the Present**

Most people miss what someone is saying or fail to hear and understand because they are distracted by something that has caught their attention. We jokingly call Squirrel Syndrome, and I'm sure you've experienced it. You are talking with someone, get distracted, and then your attention comes back, but you realize you missed a good portion of what they said. They were right in front of you, but you didn't see them or hear them while you were distracted. The noise from the conversation might have been distant or like white-noise if you were aware of it at all.

If someone's mind wanders to a past event, the emotions felt during the event resurface and show up in the present distorting our current state. It doesn't matter whether the feelings are positive or negative. It's the same with the future. If your mind wanders to the future and you imagine something happening, your current state is influenced by the feelings or emotions that arise. Again, it doesn't matter whether the thoughts are pleasant or troubling.

The listener needs to stay in the present to accurately perceive what someone is saying. They should pay close attention until they receive the full impact of the speaker's message before deciding how to respond.

It may be tough to do but staying out of the past means letting bygones be bygones.

**Be an Adult**

When I work with grade school kids teaching them the use of a Talking Stick, I inform them that making faces, or noises of disagreement while someone is speaking isn't allowed. I make a couple of faces myself, and they think it is hilarious. It goes for adults too. There is an excellent story in Chapter 8 – Stories and Examples where everyone, including me, had a tough time remaining adult.

A listener should keep a relaxed poker face even when the most absurd comments come up. Someone who rolls his or her eyes is not showing a desire to resolve an issue or be respectful.

See Chapter 8 - /The Story of Maynard and Steve

**Keep an Open Mind**

The next two stories, There's Never Just One Way to Do Anything and Walking Around the Wheel stress the importance of the designated listener keeping an open mind for several reasons:

- The tension caused by resisting the natural energy flow and the negativity of a closed mind changes the surrounding atmosphere and is felt by all participants even if they aren't conscious of it.

- A closed mind is a distraction that prevents a listener from hearing what is said just being in the past or future.

- If the designated listener shuts down and doesn't keep an open mind, they will have a tough time repeating what, if anything, they understood.

See Chapter 8 – /There's Never Only One Way to Do Anything
See Chapter 8 – /Walking Around the Wheel

**Walk in the Speaker's Shoes**

Most people have heard the saying, "You will never understand someone until you have walked a mile in their shoes." As the designated listener, walk a mile in the speaker's shoes. It is more than listening.

If the designated listener is serious about understanding, they need to shift their perspective to see a completely different view. It is one thing to look from another place on the wheel as the Walk Around the Wheel story indicates, but to be able to empathize with why the person has that view is another.

Rule 7 in the Rules of Engagement states: All opinions are valid. We all have different belief systems. We were raised differently and had diverse backgrounds. We had different parents, siblings, teachers, experiences. Some of us learned at early ages that the world was a beautiful place and others that we should never trust anyone because everyone was out to get us. Some of us had everything we desired and more than enough to eat, and others saw only poverty. Even identical twins raised together have different frames of reference, but every single person believes their opinion is valid and we have a right to our perspective.

**Promoting Respect and Boosting Self-esteem**

Obtaining a level of empathy doesn't mean changing your opinion. But this insight brings respect for the speaker's frame of reference and an understanding of why they may feel their opinion is valid. Note that empathy is not sympathy. Empathy means having an affinity with or appreciation for something, while sympathy is feeling sorry for someone and actually produces negative energy.

Whether we reach the desired result or not, a Talking Stick is a tremendous success if we promote respect on both sides or all the way around a wheel.

The Rules of Engagement are designed to boost self-esteem from Rule 1, which promises that when you speak someone will take the time to understand what you had to say because it matters, all the way to the Rule 10, which promises that what you say will be kept in strictest confidence by those participating.

**Trauma – Drama Repeating Keywords, But Not Mimicking**

It's a fine line. Most of the time the listener couldn't repeat the speaker's words verbatim even if they tried, but if they could it's probably not wise. The speaker might see it as being mimicked and take it as the listener creating drama. Also, repeating word for word indicates a great memory, but says nothing about whether the message was understood.

The second fine line is similar words. Using a word that you believe is similar may be okay but could be construed negatively. Consider using the speaker's keywords to show empathy and understanding. Here's an example:

Bob is the speaker and states he was upset when he learned he'd been passed over for a promotion. If the designated listener, Joe, responds with, "Bob, I understood you to say you were hurt…"

In a thesaurus, the word hurt is a synonym of upset but has a connotation that some may see as more emotional. Bob could be offended and feel Joe is making fun of him or exaggerating. It may not be Joe's intention, but how Bob takes it may make the situation worse. It could be safer for Joe to respond with the same keyword Bob used saying, "Bob, I heard you say that you were upset when you didn't get the promotion …." Hearing his word repeated may help Bob feel Joe understands.

Talking Sticks are designed to create better communication. We should try to improve weak communication skills when possible.

**Trauma – Drama Queen**

Listener and speaker rules of etiquette recommend staying away from anything that would cause drama during a Talking Stick. Below is one example of how a listener can remain in control when dealing with a speaker drama queen.

From an early age many people were unable or not allowed to express their needs, wants, and desires. They found they could exaggerate circumstances to get what they wanted, at least some of the time. As adults, they may still be in the dark that this is an inferior method of relationship communication.

Suggesting or blatantly stating something is exaggerated only adds fuel to the fire and does nothing to resolve an argument. It is also a violation of Rule 2 of the Rules of Engagement: The environment of a Talking Stick should always be one of respect, and Rule 8: Where a resolution is required, all participants should agree to resolve the issue for the highest good of all parties.

Responding with, "John is blowing this way out of proportion," or "Bob says that John is really blowing this out of proportion, is a violation of Rule 6: Participants must always speak using "I" statements. In both examples, the participant is speaking for someone other than themselves.

In situations when someone is trying to stir up the pot intentionally, take the higher ground. First, the designated listener should try to ignore the allegation, if possible, and respond to the remaining part of the message. That may diffuse the situation.

If it isn't possible and the speaker indicates they aren't going to back down forcing the listener to repeat a second time, the listener should answer with complete calm, "There are two sides to every story. I don't remember it happening quite that way. I'd like you to hear my view. May I share it with you when I am the speaker?"

By asking permission, two things have happened:

- the listener is indicating as politely as possible that they are not going to engage in the speaker's game playing, and

- If the speaker says *okay*, they are implying they will listen to the other side without interruption.

**The Speaker Tries to Sway Your Opinion**

If a listener feels uncomfortable or coerced in some way by a speaker, a reply such as this is recommended, "I understood your opinion is … That is not my opinion, but I believe everyone has the right to their own opinion. When I am the speaker, I will be glad to share my view, and I hope you will respect it."

**Take Notes if Allowed**

If agreeable to everyone, jot down a few keywords especially when listeners are just learning or nervous. Notes should be as brief as possible, and this is not the time to write a response to the speaker's message.

# Chapter 8
# Stories and Examples

## *Guarantee You Are Understood Lighter Side*

These are the **MisUnderstood Grannies**.

**Gerty**   **Ruby**   **Velma**   **Midge**

## *Personal/Family Sessions*

### The Youngest Talking Stick Facilitator

Dirk, a good friend of mine's son, was five years old when he overheard his parents in a heated discussion. Standing on tiptoe, he managed to get the talking stick down from the fireplace mantle and carried it to the kitchen where the argument was in progress. Dirk tugged on his mother's pant leg and held up the stick. Neither of his parents heard him coming, and his mother stared down embarrassed that her son had witnessed their squabble.

He eagle-eyed them until he had their full attention, and then sternly admonished, "You need a Talking Stick, and I will be the fish eater."

"You want to do what?" asked his father.

Irritated, Dirk repeated his statement a few decibels louder. "You need a Talking Stick, and I will be the fish eater."

The tension dissipated as their focus shifted and they began to laugh. "You want to be a fish eater, Dirk?" asked his amused mother.

"Yes, I want to be the fish eater, the fish eater, the fish eater." He stomped his small foot.

Suddenly his father got it. "Oh my gosh, he wants to be the officiator."

"That's what I said," replied Dirk.

As far as I know, Dirk is the youngest Talking Stick facilitator ever, and from what I heard, he did an excellent job. His parents had made assumptions that had no validity, and through the Talking Stick process, it became quite clear to them both. The situation could have festered and turned into something significant. I am sorry that I haven't stayed in touch with these folks. Dirk should be 26 years old as I do this rewrite.

**Best Friends Nancy and Sue**

Two women, Nancy and Sue, have been best friends and confided in each other for years. When Sue hears through the grapevine that her private issues are now common knowledge amongst several of their acquaintances, she believes the information could only have come from one source, Nancy. She is crushed and obsesses for several days imagining the worst. She asks herself: Did she do it out of spite because of something I did? Is this the end of our relationship? Can I ever forgive her for betraying my trust? Finally, she calls Nancy, and the conversation goes something like this:

"Hi, Nancy. How's the corporate world treating you?"

"Oh, hi, Sue. Wow, this week has been chaotic. I like my new boss but getting used to the new regime is going to take some time. I'm having trouble with two of my subordinates too. I think they were both hoping for my job. It's causing lots of tension, and I'm trying very hard to be tactful and win them over. Anyway, how's it going with you?"

Since Nancy seems entirely at ease, Sue feels nothing was malicious, but still wants to get to the bottom of the matter. "I know you will work things out. You always do. Hey, I heard something this week, and I need to talk to you about it."

In a worried tone, Nancy answers, "What's wrong? Are you okay? Talk to me."

"Well, I need to think more about it. I'm not sure what I need. Just hearing your voice has helped. Can we do one of those Talking Sticks that you and I read about?"

"Sure," replies Nancy. "If you're asking for a Talking Stick then I guess I guess I get to choose the place if I remember right? My house is fine if that's what you want."

"Well, they suggested a neutral location."

"Oh, yeah. Well, my second thought is Michael's Restaurant, but how about the park and then we won't be interrupted by waiters? We can get something to eat after if you want."

Sue answers, "That works. I'll have my thoughts together better when I get there, and I'll see you in our usual spot. Around 7:00?"

Within the first few seconds of their phone conversation, Sue hears the easy-going tone of her friend and realizes it wasn't malicious. Maybe Nancy wasn't aware this was a sensitive issue. But, before they meet at the park, Sue needs to decide what she wants as a result. Will Sue be satisfied with just telling Nancy that her feelings were hurt? Or, is she looking for amends?

Here is an excellent example of why planning is necessary. I was in a session where a woman told her husband that he had hurt her feelings. He gave her a meaningful apology and then he looked to her for the next step. She had no idea what to do next, so she just reiterated her point. Before it was over her husband was angry because it appeared that all the session for was to complain.

**Nancy's Opening at the Park**

"Thanks for agreeing to this, Sue. I know I've acted strangely this week. I've wanted to do an actual Talking Stick ever since you and I heard about them and the second reason is that I don't know what to think about something I heard Shawn and Ashley discussing. It was about me, and there's only one way they could know about it, and that would have been to hear it from you. It's upset me. I hope you'll hear me out."

With this opening, Sue knows what to expect. If she is still in agreement to proceed, Nancy is the one who starts the dialog.

# *Welcoming Sessions*

**A Sisterhood Welcoming Session**

I was a member of a sisterhood group of women back around 2000. The leader would pass the talking stick to establish the collective, but with no additional instruction, the process spurred some of the women to complain about something every month; their husbands were doing something they didn't like, or the kids were at it again.

Instead of enjoying the Welcoming, I found myself dreading it. I suggested the leader have each woman say something she had done for herself during the past month (that didn't include the husband or kids). The result was amazing. The energy changed dramatically and became much more upbeat.

The leader begins the dialog giving an example of their idea and passes the stick when they are done using proper protocol or etiquette.

**Break the Ice or Get Down to Business?**

I knew Janet while I lived in California. She and I chatted over lunch one day about a corporate event that her boss wanted her to plan. Two years before, the corporate parent had purchased two smaller companies and for some executives, this was going to be the first time they had met in person. Everyone knew that during the weekend the board would have to make some serious decisions, but Janet hated to throw everyone into an atmosphere of doom and gloom on Friday evening while they were still putting names to faces.

The question she asked was, "Should I just *break the ice* and help everyone become acquainted or get down to business right from the beginning?"

She opted for the ice-breaker Welcoming and added the desired result of *telling something no one knew about them*. It created a lighthearted beginning, and she said she felt several people give a big sigh of relief when they realized the serious business wasn't going to start until Saturday. She said she heard one out-of-town exec say they'd received a stay of execution.

Base your purpose and desired results on the amount of time allowed and how well the participants know each other. And even if it is a reunion of old friends, it is great to welcome individuals and set the direction and objective.

### Who Moved the Chocolate?

You've probably read or at least heard of the *a-mazing* book about a poor mouse in a maze having to deal with stress and change when he finds his cheese is missing. *Who Moved My Cheese?* by Spencer Johnson is a classic.

A Life Coach friend did workshops with a similar scenario but then extended the fun with exercises over a long weekend. She called the seminar *Who Moved the Chocolate*, which was perfect for the professional women attending.

She kicked off the Friday evening get-together with a chocolate fondue fountain and a Talking Stick Welcoming that included all the women introducing themselves and describing their favorite chocolate delicacy. The women were told in advance to bring the recipes, and during the event, my friend's staff compiled them along with other handouts into an adorable giveaway. Of course, the rewards for winning competitions and games was chocolate.

## *Brainstorming Sessions*

### Brainstorming for the Holidays

There were employees at United that remembered when Holiday Parties were at fancy downtown hotels with filet mignon and open bar lunches. There were even earlier years that included formal evening dining and dancing with spouses, but for the last five years since Renee, the VP of Human Resources had been on the job, the parties had been potluck lunches with Santa Steal gift exchanges and the afternoon off.

Now, once again, there was money to be spent, and Renee had the green light for an actual corporate party. She felt the weight of the whole company on her shoulders when she realized they were expecting this event to bring back the spirit of the glory years. She knew two things: Twenty years was a long time ago and she wasn't about to copy a party from back when some employees were five years old. Second, every department was going to help her.

She sent me her story in 2012. She organized a Talking Stick and invited the oldest person, the youngest person, and the receptionist from each department. They brainstormed for two hours, had a ball and came up with over sixty ideas for locations, entertainment, food, attire, gimmicks (it was 2012, and no one knew whether the world would be ending or not), door prizes, and several families to support for the holidays.

From the collection of ideas, they selected a location entirely different from anything available twenty years previous and managed to accommodate most of the plans. The site was called Pinstripes and uniquely had a ballroom for the sit-down dinner, plus a separate bar, bistro, bowling, and bocce ball area for those that chose to roam instead of taking advantage of the live music and dancing. Renee said in her email that she would never have selected the location without the help of the brainstormers and she doubted the event would have been as successful.

**Wheel of Fortune FABs**

Imagine a brainstorming session conducted like Wheel of Fortune with me as Vanna White. I met, Mike, a director in a direct sales travel business through an event I promoted on parent/teen communication.

We hit it off, and I wasn't surprised when he called later and asked if I would facilitate a Talking Stick at one of their annual events. I expected it to be a welcoming session, but instead it was something unique. He wanted me to host a game designed to help new salespeople understand the concept of and differences between features, advantages, and benefits of their business (this turned out to be the desired result).

I was old enough to be familiar with FABs, which went back to 1975 and Zig Ziglar training. The concept, of course, is that features are characteristics of a product/service, advantages are why that product/service is favored or superior, and benefits are the actual *what's in it for me* (sometimes called WIIFM) and the reason people buy. His staff could not grasp the concept that consumers don't buy features and advantages, they buy benefits.

I love challenges, and I had a copy of what the final document/desired result was supposed to look like, so that's where I started. Below is a very abbreviated version; the real one was four pages.

### FABs for XYZ Direct Marketing (abbreviated final version)

| Features | Advantages | Benefits |
|---|---|---|
| Home-based business. | Don't work to make someone else rich; work for yourself. | Freedom, job security, get to fire your boss. |
| Baby Boomers as clients. | One Boomer will retire every 8 sec for the next 20 years. | Millions of people are going to have the freedom to travel. |
| The Internet is the foundation. | Can be accessed from anywhere. | You have a source that connects the world to your fingertips. |
| Travel industry. | $7 trillion industry that is expected to grow to $14 trillion in next 10 yrs. | XYZ has only scratched the surface of the market with ½ of 1% penetration. |

| No normal small business headaches. | No inventory, no employees, no accounting, no collections, no quotes. | You are free to work your business and not work *at* your business. |
|---|---|---|
| Part time, full time, new career. | You have a Plan B that can become Plan A. | Build your business at the speed that is right for you and your family. |
| Millions of dollars of inventory. | Booking engine holds inventory. Not in your garage. No packing, shipping, FedEx. | People already travel. Get them to change the way they book it. It's FREE for them. |

Our planning came down to this: The desired result was for all salespeople to leave with a copy of the final document they created, and to understand the concept above. The game would end (barometer indicator reached) when they completed the last of the boxes correctly.

Five large whiteboards were brought in and placed around the room. Masking tape was used to create grids on each. Mike was to give a brief lesson on the topic and then pass out a jumbled sheet with only the top row correct, plus blank sheets. See below. I would give brief opening remarks and instructions for passing the talking stick (popcorn style) and place it in the middle.

The first participant to figure out the correct placement of one of the text boxes, could come forward get the stick, explain their reasoning (speaker) and then write it on one of the boards (speaker finished). If it was a feature, someone else could add the advantage or benefit next but would have to be the designated listener first and discuss further or repeat the speaker's message about the feature (Guarantee), then they would become the new speaker and talk about what text they were going to add. The rotation could be willy-nilly, but all the text boxes needed filling, and a Guarantee accomplished for each speaker.

**FABs for XYZ Direct Marketing Game (abbreviated version)**

| Features | Advantages | Benefits |
|---|---|---|
| Home-based business. | Don't work to make someone else rich; work for yourself. | Freedom, job security, get to fire your boss. |
| You have a Plan B that can become Plan A. | The Internet is foundation. | $7 trillion industry that is expected to grow to $14 trillion in next 10 yrs. |
| You are free to work your business and not work "at" your business. | People already travel. Get them to change the way they book it. It's FREE for them. | Baby Boomers as clients. |
| XYZ has only scratched the surface of the market with ½ of 1% penetration. | You have a source that connects the world at your fingertips. | Booking engine holds inventory. Not in your garage. No packing, shipping, FedEx. |
| No inventory, no employees, no accounting, no collections, no quotes. | Build your business at the speed that is right for you and your family. | One Boomer will retire every 8 sec for the next 20 years. |
| Millions of people are going to have the freedom to travel. | No normal small business headaches. | Part time, full time, new career. |
| Can be accessed from anywhere. | Travel industry. | Millions of dollars of inventory. |

It turned out to be an incredible educational tool, and everyone had loads of fun in the process. The winner, who placed the most text, got a 3-day cruise to the Bahamas.

I asked Mike at the end about where he got the *Wheel of Fortune* aspect. I said, "There wasn't a wheel." He answered, "Sure there was. Everyone in the room was sitting on one."

## *Fact Finding Sessions*

### The Home-court Advantage

A friend's son kept getting in trouble in school. The fourth-grade teacher punished him several times, but it was apparent that was not the solution. They felt there was more to the incidents than the teacher was telling them, and they wanted to hear their son's side of the story without him becoming defensive. He needed to be in the right frame of mind for the discussion, and a neutral location was imperative. They chose the giant sandbox that had been his refuge for many years when he was younger. He got a big kick out of them joining him on his turf, and the session had a positive start. He was relaxed and open, and they learned a great deal about how to help their son that day.

I knew some parents who chose a place where the family had enjoyed spending time together believing it would be ideal but during the process, their daughter revealed issues that no one was expecting. The family was glad everything was out in the open, but the mom mentioned they needed to find a new favorite place.

**Just Getting the Facts**

I helped a medical reimbursement consulting firm establish a new office in 1994. The owner, Charly, loved people, had no trouble signing new medical offices as clients. He was not a detail man though and hired a young woman, Chris, to run the processing department. She had expertise in medical coding and was a whiz with computers. She did so well that Charly almost forgot about that end of the business. He told everyone she was a wizard, and he took off and played golf with the clients.

Chris was very talented at what she did but quite inexperienced in other areas. When the first problem arose, she tried to deal with it and was reluctant to mention anything to Charly for fear of lessening his opinion of her. The situation compounded and when it couldn't be kept under wraps any longer, fingers began pointing in all directions between the five-person staff. Charly was utterly in the dark as to what had happened.

Over breakfast, I heard about the mess and suggested a Fact Finding session. The office was closed the next morning to sort things out. The atmosphere was subdued when I got there. Charly opened the meeting by apologizing for dropping the ball and asked to be brought up to date. His demeanor put everyone at ease, and I realized there was no real animosity amongst the staff, everyone was just worried their job might be in jeopardy.

After the staff had their say, I suggested we turn the process into a Brainstorming session and look for solutions. They agreed. Charly slipped out and ordered pizza. I closed out the first session. Everyone grabbed a slice and a soda, and the atmosphere changed to one of excitement and anticipation. The challenge was a good one; the business had grown so fast they hadn't kept up. In the beginning, the only employee needed was Chris. As Charly brought in more business individuals with medical coding experience were hired, but no one had office management experience.

Charly immediately agreed to handle the initial problem and realized he needed a full-time office manager for the future. Two possible candidates surfaced during the session, and he arranged to interview them the next week. He said if they needed someone for customer service, he'd have the office manager handle that. He asked everyone to promise never to let matters get entirely out of hand again.

Several of the staff thanked me that afternoon and Chris approached me in tears. That was when I found out that if we hadn't done the Talking Stick, she would have resigned before the end of the day.

## *Difficult Discussions*

**Two Sets of Rules**

Sam, a friend's son, cheated on a science midterm and I don't know if it was guilt or his fearful expectations, but he asked his parents for a Talking Stick that evening. His parents told him they were proud of him for coming clean, but the punishment for anything like that in the future would be losing cell phone privileges for a month. They also suggested he confess to his teacher. It would be Sam's decision, and whether he did or didn't, they could not protect him from the school's rules if they found out.

Sam did confess and took an F without any further discipline. Sam's mom told me the part that hurt the most was that his overall grade for the class dropped from an A to a C and kept him from competing in a debate championship.

**Amy's Eating Disorder**

A family whose daughter was anorexic asked for my help. Drew and Suan knew Amy had an eating disorder but believed she was much better since she had started Overeaters Anonymous. When she came home from college for a holiday vacation, they realized she had relapsed and was indeed at her bottom, weighing only ninety-five pounds. They wanted her to go into a treatment center, but her reaction to this in the past had been strong resistance.

Because of several comments Amy made, I knew she considered a treatment center to be punishment for her actions. I told Drew and

Suan that I would not facilitate to help coerce Amy, but that I would be glad to assist if the purpose was to get Amy to find her solution and regain her abstinence. She wasn't 18, but close to it. They reluctantly agreed to allow her one more chance but wanted to state in the session that if her solution did not work by itself, she would enter a treatment center. This scenario complied with the rules of engagement.

During the session, Amy talked about several of her friend's parents who regularly went to Al-Anon meetings. Drew and Suan believed Al-Anon was only for alcoholics, but now that they knew, they were happy to go and Amy's self-esteem rose when she realized they trusted her. Amy agreed to get back to work on the twelve steps of the program, and even her sister volunteered to go to Al-A-Teen. There was a dramatic change in Drew and Suan also as they watched their daughter take charge of her life. The last I heard Amy had not relapsed.

**Nicos and Erin**

Erin and Nicos fell in love and married in one of California's open-minded communities. Nicos was Catholic, and Erin grew up with Native American/Pagan/Wiccan teachings. When the families got together, there were 4th of July fireworks. Both sets of parents had preconceived notions about the other's spirituality. They finally agreed through Erin's tears and Nico's threats of never seeing grandchildren, to sit down to a Talking Stick session.

The Difficult Discussion session intended that neither side could bring up grievances and could only speak of the significant aspects of their spirituality, namely history, and beliefs. No one converted that day as was expected, but both sides left with an appreciation of the other's values and a much better understanding of how their children could have fallen in love. They also had a new willingness (and even a touch of anticipation) to share in each other's holidays and traditions.

**The Italian Mother-in-Law**

Tony married a beautiful woman named Grace. The first Christmas the couple was together they invited both Tony's mother and Grace's, and there was Italian/Irish friction from the start. They got through Christmas Eve, but by 4:00 pm on Christmas Day 1998, the delectable sit-down dinner had turned into a food fight with flying cranberries and pumpkin pie. Tony managed to stay out of the fray, but Grace was sucked in and no matter what she did, was on the wrong side with both mothers for the next five years.

After Tony's mother died, he wanted to plan a surprise Talking Stick to get Grace and her mother back together. The ruse was that a woman in Tony's office was having a make-up party (pun intended). He wanted me to facilitate. First, I told him that it was trickery and I was sure it violated several Rules of Engagement. Second, if it didn't work, he still had to live with his wife. He backed off the surprise issue and genuinely told each how much it would mean to him if they would "make up" for real. Considering the history, I wondered if this Talking Stick was doomed from the beginning but was willing to give it a shot. The timing was right for both women. The death of Tony's mother reminded both how precarious life was, and they shouldn't be wasting another minute apart.

## *Conflict Resolution Sessions*

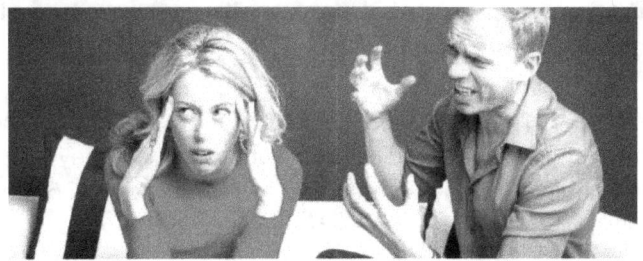

**Joyce and Don's Child Custody Session**

Two friends of mine in another state were divorcing, and the circumstances over child custody were messy. Joyce repeatedly tried to discuss issues over the phone with her husband, Don, but the calls escalated into substantial screaming matches. She decided a Talking Stick might be a solution but didn't want to be alone with her husband. She consulted with me, and I recommended a facilitator if Don was to take her seriously, but it was impossible for me to get there.

Through a chain of strange events, they agreed to ask a Jewish rabbi, who was a friend of a friend to both Joyce and Don. It was the first thing they had agreed on in a year. I told Joyce it was a sign. The rabbi had never heard of a Talking Stick but was glad to participate. I sent him the first version of this book, and he caught on quickly. He organized the session and prepared for a safe and civil discussion. Joyce told me they got issues resolved for a change. The rabbi was impressed and continues with Talking Stick processes today. We have shared experiences several times over the phone.

### Joyce's Opening for the Child Custody Session

Joyce said she began the session with something like this: Don, thanks for agreeing to this. I hope this is a turning point and that you and I can have more Talking Sticks on our own in the future. Nothing against you, rabbi, but you're probably not always available on Saturday evenings, but I'm delighted you agreed today. (chuckle) Don, I know you love the kids very much, and I know you want the best for them. I want to share why I feel they should change schools next year and show you that it doesn't have anything to do with the new job that I just got or that it appears that it is going to make things easier for me. Once you've heard me out, I believe you will see that you may benefit from the change more than I will.

Joyce told me this was the longest she had been able to speak without being interrupted in five years. She said that whether they made it through all the points, she wanted to cover in the session or not, getting this statement out was tremendous progress.

**Town Council Mediation in Colorado**

I facilitated a Talking Stick for a town council in Colorado that was somewhat unique. The board included more than a dozen successful businesses and some enormous egos. The Mayor was a good friend of my husband, and he asked if I would consider trying something different to unlock a gridlocked issue. A Talking Stick was very different and, in the beginning, not well received.

In the case of the Colorado Town Council, we made several attempts to get the group interested to no avail, until I decided to appeal to their egos and sent them a copy of the questionnaire that appears in Appendix G – Questions for Utilizing Strengths of the Participants.4 They were more than willing to tell me what they felt were their strengths. The only challenge was rating the statements from 1 to 8 with 1 being their greatest strength and 8 being their least. Several wanted 1s in every box.

It took two sessions to resolve the issues, but after the first, I knew it was going to happen. The significance was that fifteen influential individuals decided to respect the Rules of Engagement, put their issues aside and work for the greater good of the community. I realized I had glimpsed how the Iroquois Confederacy had managed to remain at peace for 700 years.

---

[4] This form is used by certified Guarantee You Are Understood Facilitators and Coaches. If you have an interest, check Appendix B for more information.

**Town Council Mediation Introduction**

The opening for the town council mediation I did in Colorado went something like this:

Mayor Johnson: I want to welcome you all here tonight. I appreciate the work that so many have put into making this happen. In just a few minutes I am going to turn this over to Phyllis Cronbaugh who will facilitate this historic Talking Stick session. (chuckles) Before I do, I want to say that I've believed in this new business area/park/open space and the value it will have for our community since long before I became mayor. The fact that we haven't been able to come together as a community and agree on how to get it done has given me many sleepless nights. I hope this session tonight is our answer.

Because of the facilities offered by the surrounding town's revenue is stolen from our local shop owners every day. This project will funnel that business back into their pockets. I know you'll be discussing the trade-offs tonight and what I ask is that you put your issues aside and think of what is best for our town. The voters elected you to represent them and not yourself. Thank you. And, now I introduce Phyllis Cronbaugh to those of you who don't know her.

**The Trade Show Conflict**

Here is a situation where I was called in to facilitate. It covers a Fact Finding, Conflict Resolution, and Difficult Discussion session.

An organization found themselves in chaos as they prepared for their first trade show. One issue centered around an individual's actions that were forcing other committee members to take sides and the group was becoming divided. The committee wasn't getting anything done at this crucial time before the big event. I was asked to facilitate a Talking Stick and, initially, everyone thought it was a good move until they realized they needed a consensus on several points before they even started.

The offending woman, as I will call her, had been a long-time member of the organization. Because of her presumed actions:

- several members wanted to hear both sides before making a decision,
- another man said he wanted to give her a warning,
- one said he wanted to get on with things – time was short – and he was ready to ask for her resignation from the committee, and
- another still said she wanted the woman to leave the organization permanently.

I told them the first decision they had to make was whether they wanted to hear the woman's side or not. This further divided them. Only two of the members had used a talking stick before, and they weren't well versed in the Rules of Engagement. Here was my advice:

- If they were going to ask the woman to leave based on what they currently knew, they didn't need a Talking Stick. They could do it and hope there were no repercussions.

- If they wanted to hear everyone's opinion during a Talking Stick, including the offending woman, the group could ask her to leave, but not as part of the session. Rule 9 states: Participants will never receive discipline as a direct result of something that is said or revealed during a Talking Stick.

  If the woman participated, the group could discuss consequences if behavior or conduct did not change but could not act on it at that time. It would have to be a warning.

They decided it was only fair to get more information because of her longevity with the organization, so they voted to have a session.

We laid out a three-part process:

1. They would start with a Fact Finding session and the Q&A Combo format. The group would ask the offending woman questions to bring everyone up to date.

2. The woman would leave for the next process. We would close out the Fact Finding session, take a quick break and open a Conflict Resolution session. One person was

designated to state the results from the first session. The group would decide their recourse if the behavior did not change.

3. The Conflict Resolution process would end, there would be a ten-minute break, the woman would return, and a Difficult Discussion session would begin. The woman would hear the group's decision, and the stick would go around one last time for final remarks.

I recommended recording the session to set timing restrictions. See Timer and Recorder below for the details. Nine individuals were going to participate, and each could speak twice for no more than four minutes each time. They expected the first part to be complete within 90 minutes. They allocated 30 minutes for the second part and 30 minutes for the third part.

Without initial planning and considerations, the organization could have opened itself up to further damage and repercussions. If they had started a Talking Stick on their own, the individuals who wanted to kick the offending woman out of the committee would probably have started a war with those who wished clarification, and the offending woman would have been in the middle watching the ball bounce back and forth in amazement, which would have accomplished nothing.

Depending on the organization and the litigious environment we live in, without some precautions the group might have opened themselves up for legal action from the offending woman or others in the group.

**The Fifteen-step Action Plan**

I did some mediation for a security tech firm in California in 2003 to help the partners make decisions regarding the sale of their company. I got to know their production manager, Jacob, well. A few months later they contracted with a consultant, Joanne, who had expertise in business valuation to help with the process. There was immediate tension between her and several of the management team. The vice-president who had recommended me told Jacob to organize a Talking Stick; it had worked before.

Whether Joanne purposefully sabotaged the session or was just too busy to learn the process is still unknown. She claimed to know the Rules of Engagement, but according to Jacob, she didn't read past Rule 1. He said, "She missed the part on respect, the rule on resolving something for the highest good, the one about criticism and judgment and several more. And, somehow she missed the rule about only talking when you have the stick."

When Joanne was the speaker, she quickly rattled off fifteen steps in an action plan. As designated speaker, Jacob missed several, and she took offense, took the stick back and rudely told him to start over. Jacob immediately took it as an intimidation tactic, but tried again, trying to keep an attitude of respect. To make a long story short. The session went downhill and ended awkwardly. Joanne even refused to vote to give the process a Stalemate status. This event might have ended differently if there had been a facilitator, but hindsight is always 20-20.

Joanne's contract was canceled the following week for several reasons, and Jacob said the ordeal was an excellent lesson on how a qualified leader should prepare for and lead a session, and that he believed in the need for Talking Sticks more than ever.

**Mutiny in Arizona**

The reason for this story is two-fold: It describes reasons why I decided to *pass on my right to speak* during a Talking Stick, and it's also a story of standing up for and protecting what you believe.

There are many reasons why someone would pass on their right to speak. If you are complete and have nothing more to say then moving on is a blessing because taking up everyone's time when you have nothing to say is rather rude. You might also pass because you found yourself involved in something you hadn't expected.

Years ago I was asked to help out in a Difficult Discussion session:

We weren't given a lot of direction before the Talking Stick began and I wasn't sure what to expect or where it was going. On the first round, I spoke somewhat philosophically about several issues, but by the time the stick came back around to me again the mud had started to fly with the real purpose for the session.

I had been at the event and witnessed the activity causing the chaos now. I'd made no judgments at the time because I hadn't known the background. It didn't seem that much of an issue. It sounded more like a dispute between two strong personalities. The second round brought veiled accusations between two individuals, and it was quite childish and stupid. We'd been blindsided, and for some reason these two guys wanted us to take sides. I chose to pass because I wanted to distance myself from the circumstances and didn't feel I was doing anyone a disservice. I didn't have information that would affect the desired result.

But, by the third pass of the talking stick, I knew I had to speak, but not on the issue. Things had gotten ridiculous, and it was evident the facilitator was not going to intervene. I was furious on several counts:

- The first was false pretenses. I'd agreed to attend a Difficult Discussion session believing the purpose was one issue when in reality it was something else entirely and a Conflict Resolution session.

- Blatant disregard for the Rules of Engagement. Several of the rules were not observed. Actually, most of them and no one knew anything about etiquette.

An incompetent facilitator. There were several occasions when a good facilitator would have intervened to keep the session on track, but this one had done nothing. I wouldn't say he was biased, just incompetent.

When I had the stick, I spoke to all three of the points above. I started by asking my designated listener, "Are you ready to write? I have a lot to say." She looked at me strangely then pulled out a pen and nodded.

Even though Rule 5 states: A person can only speak when he or she has the talking stick, (When someone has the stick, others must refrain from talking, which includes all comments and gestures even when in agreement, and especially when disagreeing with the speaker.), heads were nodding and there were gestures of approval all around the circle. The three that looked the most dumbfounded were the two individuals at cross purposes and the facilitator.

My last comment was, "I would give this session an outcome status of Agreeing to Disagree, close it, and let us all go home. If you want results, I would suggest doing some planning.

## *Other Stories*

### The Fidgety Young Woman

As a facilitator, I watched a group before a session and noticed a young woman exhibiting some odd behavior. I asked her if she was okay, and she shivered a little and then assured me she was but a few minutes later she was fidgeting again and appeared very nervous. I said nothing more. The Talking Stick began, and when she became the designated listener, it was obvious her mind was elsewhere as she repeated what was understood, but the speaker said he felt complete and she became the new speaker. She stumbled and stammered through her pitch. I intuited that she was anxious about being criticized, so when the session took a break a while later, I approached and asked if I could tell her a story that I called *The Office Jerk*. She said sure. Here's the story.

Ted moved from one department to another in a large firm. During his first few days on the job, he overheard a guy bullying a woman and knew who it was even though he couldn't see the guy through the partition. Harry had quite a reputation. Ted made a mental note to stay out of Harry's way but seemed to stumble over him around every corner. Even though they never spoke, Ted felt nauseated when they were in a room together.

Then, because of his previous experience, Ted's boss asked him to participate in a Fact Finding Talking Stick along with several others and Harry. His boss would be the facilitator.

Ted almost had an anxiety attack. This event was his chance to prove to the boss that he was the right guy for the job. He wondered if his feelings for Harry would show? As offensive as it was, Ted resolved to keep an open mind concerning all the ideas, even the ones that Harry might express.

Harry grabbed the stick in the first few minutes of the popcorn-style meeting, and to Ted's amazement, the idea he expressed was brilliant and dovetailed perfectly into what he planned to propose. Several others had ideas that enhanced the process even further, and Ted could see his boss' excitement. The Talking Stick was a huge success. In the end, Ted's view of Harry as the office jerk hadn't changed, but he did have respect for Harry's business insight.

The break was over just as I finished the story, so the woman hurried back to the wheel, saying nothing else. After the session ended, she approached with a huge smile. "Wow!" she said, "As I was walking back in, I announced my intention to the Universe to be completely open-minded, and I suddenly felt all this positive energy hit me. That's the only way I can explain it. I realize now why I was so uncomfortable before. I was judging what everyone else said and assumed they were going to judge me. After the break, I said what I really wanted to say and when I looked around people were nodding in agreement. It was amazing. Thanks."

**The Story of Maynard and Steve**

Maynard and Steve attended a class I was giving and took the opportunity to ask for a Talking Stick.

They had been a couple for ten years when Steve took his dream job. The only problem was it was an hour from home, and Steve rode the Cal Train. It wasn't long before he formed friendships with several gay and straight guys that also rode daily. At the time, Maynard hadn't had the chance to meet the guys, and after a couple of occasions when Steve took late trains and came home with bar-breath, there was trouble.
Steve asked for a Talking Stick, and the trouble intensified during the session. Both had been involved in processes before, but not with each other. They knew the rules of etiquette, but they were both angry, and when the eye-rolling started they looked like five-year-olds. I was ready to call a Stalemate when the whole thing struck me as hysterical, and I started laughing and couldn't stop. They stared at me, which made me laugh harder and tears rolled down my cheeks. Finally, they were laughing too.

It was not my most professional moment, and it was definitely unintentional, but it lightened the mood and actually ended okay. When our hysteria died, we were able to complete the session.

A listener needs to keep a relaxed poker face even when the most absurd comments come up. A listener that rolls his or her eyes is not showing a desire to resolve an issue.

**Revealing Ulterior Motives**

I was asked to facilitate a session years ago by the wife of a couple I met at a backyard BBQ hosted by a good friend. The request appeared to be sincere, but I became suspicious of her motives soon after. As I was leaving, I overheard her talking on the phone, and two comments caught my attention. She said she'd arranged one of those *silly Talking Sticks* that Toni (our mutual friend) was raving about, and the second included the words, "... needs to be put in his place." I phoned her the next day under the context of asking about some arrangement, and she reassured me that no one wanted a resolution to the issue more than she.

As the session began, she spoke respectfully, and I thought I'd been wrong. When she finished, her husband started the Guarantee process and did an excellent job of repeating what he understood the issue to be. But instead of the wife agreeing and then giving him his chance to speak, she asked for the stick to be returned so she could clarify a point. It was like a switch had been flipped. She didn't explain anything but started with a series of nasty innuendos and revealed her actual intent.

I never discovered if her motive was to pick a fight in a safe place to argue or to embarrass her husband and humiliate him. Maybe in the past, she didn't have the confidence to speak up and felt that in a private session she might be less threatened. The husband seemed mild-mannered enough to me, and I had a hard time believing this was the answer. As far as humiliating him, that seemed remote also. I felt if she wanted to *put someone in their place* as I heard her say on the phone, she would choose a public location and a larger audience than just a Talking Stick facilitator.

A facilitator has several jobs; they need to keep a session on track, ensure that participants follow the Rules of Engagement, make sure the Guarantee is accomplished to the speaker's satisfaction, and encourage all participants to use appropriate Talking Stick etiquette. So, I paused the session and told her she needed to clarify whatever she felt her husband had misinterpreted and then give him a second chance to complete the Guarantee; if there were other issues she could bring them up later. She agreed but didn't change her attitude, and after one more try to get the session on target, I called it a *stalemate* much to her surprise and left picking up the check she had written for my payment on the way out the door.

In her mind maybe, she felt she'd proved her point. It was a *silly session* and didn't work to resolve her issue, but not because Talking Sticks don't work, but because she entered one without a desire to address a problem for the highest good of both parties.

See Chapter 6 – /Ending a Session When the Barometer Indicates for a definition of Stalemate.

**There's Never Only One Way to Do Anything**

When white men came to the Americas, they brought a very different type of thinking from what the native people were accustomed.

There are recorded events where natives received instruction on how to do a task. The native watched politely, nodded and then walked away with no animosity or disrespect, but kept doing whatever it was the way he always had.

The white man couldn't understand why the native didn't immediately appreciate the lesson and change, feeling his method was, of course, superior.

But, the idea that there was only one way to do something or just one way to view an issue was utterly foreign to the native. If the native didn't immediately see the white man's approach an improvement upon what he had done for millennia, why change?

**Walking Around the Wheel**

At a gathering with Native American elders in 1997, I was asked to stand with seven others in a circle or what they call a medicine wheel. I chose the south direction. There was a giant, paper-mâché sculpture in the center and the grandmother giving the lesson began asking each of us what we saw.

I reported, "I see a little green figure with eyes, antennas sticking out of the top of his head, yellow and blue shirt, pink pants, maybe a gun or taser, and a great big smile."

The grandmother said, "You're absolutely right." Then she asked the person in the north. He answered in a strange voice, "I'm not sure what Phyllis saw. I see white wings or a cape, one big eyeball and it's glaring at me. Definitely it has a gun. It's pretty scary."

The elder said, "You're absolutely right." The woman in the east reported fairy wings, a yellow and blue t-shirt, said she couldn't see eyes but saw an arm and hand with two fingers. She said, "It's standing very relaxed and appears easy going. I would say friendly."

"You're absolutely right," was the response. Someone said the green thing was standing in a shimmering mist. Another person said he wasn't smiling, it was a maniacal grin, and he had one of his fingers on the trigger. Another said a yellow spotlight was directly overhead and was ready to beam the guy up to space.

It didn't matter what we saw, what mattered was that while looking at the same object we all saw something different.

The members of the Iroquois League of Five Nations understood there are eight views (actually many more) for any object, idea, problem, or challenge. When one member had a different perspective, they understood they were standing in a different place on the wheel. They honored the other's opinion even though they may not have agreed. Honoring did not mean they changed their personal opinion, but they respected the other's view.

# Appendix A
# Make Your Own Talking Stick

In Chapter 1 – What Is a Talking Stick? Where Did They Originate? I briefly mentioned the use of talking sticks as far back as Neanderthals. Up through the ages nearly every culture has used sticks, wands, batons, or scepters as either a tool to indicate a position of power, leadership or royalty.

**Native American Traditions**

> Talking Sticks embody the heart-wisdom
> of the tribal family, and are often artifacts
> of great beauty, simplicity, or significance.
> They spiritually empower the holder to speak
> his or her truth as an offering
> to another person or the tribe.
> Cherokee elder.

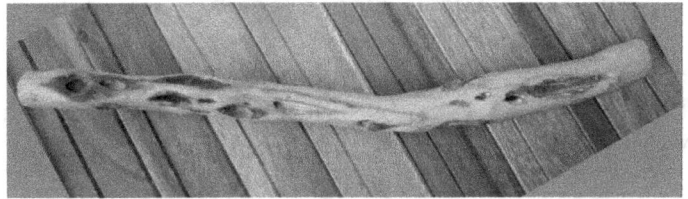

The Diamond Willow branch above could be picked up in the woods and used as a talking stick at any time. There are no rules for making a talking stick. They are as individual as the speakers and listeners who will use them. If a situation arises and you feel the need to have a Talking Stick session immediately, a pen or pencil or some other object at hand can work fine. Some, groups today pass a feather to honor the indigenous people who are given credit for introducing the tradition to America.

Chapter 1 in the original book began with: …the mystery and magick of the talking stick are where truth occurs – the manifestation of true heart-to-heart communication.

The spelling of the word magick above is correct. Today magic means *sleight of hand*. The ancients didn't have a word for this. If they did it would probably be considered trickery, which wouldn't necessarily have been bad for most Native Americans were known for their love of gambling and being pranksters. The word magick stems from magi, which were ancient priests, wizards or sorcerers who had the gift of creating alchemical change or change at the cellular level, which native people believe happens when souls connect.

In 2012, I struck an agreement with a Korean publishing company for the rights to translate the original book into Korean. A picture of their cover is in the Prologue. Whether they got the idea for their cover art from that first paragraph or somewhere else, I have no idea, but their art indicates what the Western world today would call a magic wand. The complete story of how the transaction occurred is available on the website.

**Use Your Imagination**

If you can feel the magic, black top hats are available in magic stores and can create a fun environment for a session. Also, with the popularity of Harry Potter, you have access to some fantastic wands that are available on Amazon.com or elsewhere (stick to the light side). Or if you wish to create your own, here are some ideas taken from Native Peoples. Let your imagination go wild.

Use a stick between 15" and 18" in length. You can use a dowel rod, or a branch found in the woods. Driftwood makes beautiful talking sticks. It can be straight or gnarly with lots of knotholes. Please, don't cut a live branch from a tree, but if that is your only choice, use a native tradition and thank the tree after you remove the limb. You can leave it a gift of tobacco (not a cigarette with a filter, just the tobacco), some cornmeal, a hair from your head, or some spit or saliva.

My late husband was a woodcarver, and I made a pair of talking sticks from a walking stick that he carved. I cut it in half and used the top for my stepdaughter and the bottom half for myself. My stepdaughter's features a rustic impression of a mountain man and I began a beading pattern using circular peyote stitch below the carving. My half continues the beading pattern keeping the connection.

An old Arizona gold miner and historian gifted me a saguaro cactus spine. I decorated it with trade beads, turquoise, porcupine quills, and leather fringe.

I've made numerous sticks from ¾" diameter dowel rods beading them with the peyote stitch. Most became gifts for friends.

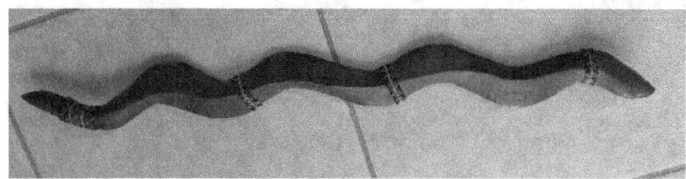

A friend found a carved snake in a thrift store. He gave it to me believing it might be a nice medicine gift to thank someone for doing a sweat lodge ceremony. I beaded it using a rattlesnake pattern. Maybe I will give it away someday, or perhaps not.

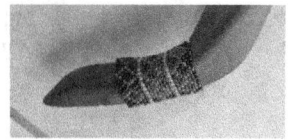

While walking the shores of a lake one day, I found a piece of driftwood. The top is bent over and looks exactly like the head of a dragon. It didn't take much to make it into a talking stick. All I had to do was add a large red crystal stone for the eye.

My maiden name was Murphy, and my father was very proud of a real Irish shillala given to him years ago. Shillalas are weapons of old. When he crossed over, I took it and made it into a talking stick using a rainbow bead pattern. It's a great conversation piece and will never be used again in war.

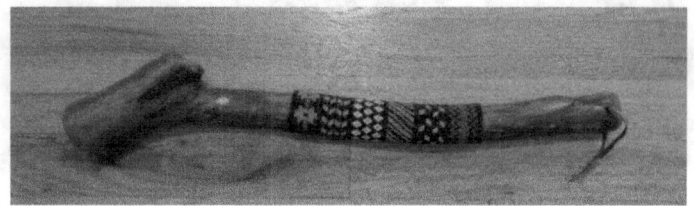

The stick below was a gift from an amazing artist for facilitating a ceremony. It is made from a very thick grapevine (about an inch and a half in diameter). Attached to one end is smoky quartz crystal that is also a geode. See the hole in the crystal, which is lined with a dozen more crystals.

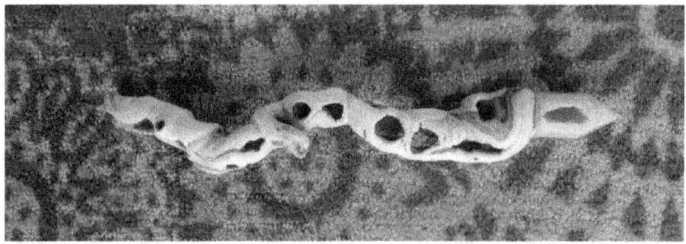

**Making Your Talking Stick using Native Traditions**

Native People say the four Worlds of Grandmother (or Mother) Earth surround them – Mineral, Plant, Animal, and Human. If you choose a Native motif, include something from each of the worlds. You may want to add the Spirit World or Ancestor World as well. When you hold the stick, you represent the Human World.

The stick itself represent the Plant World, but you can wrap it additionally with sweetgrass braids, add sage, cedar, or any flower.

The beading that I have done uses size 11 seed beads to create intricate circular patterns in what is called peyote or brick stitch. Most craft stores have books that teach this beading pattern. You may choose to bead straight onto the stick or add leather first and secure your beading to it. Beading straight onto the piece allows you to slip the beaded area up and down and is great if you aren't sure where your pattern may take you; beading onto leather which is glued to the stick is more permanent. You can also use a beading loom to create a long strip and wrap it around the wood. Both are beautiful. Since most seed beads are glass, they are a representation of the Mineral World. Hobby stores carry beads, but generally not the highest quality. They may work for some projects, but intricate patterns call for beads that are precisely symmetrical. Better quality beads can be purchased online or through catalogs like Fire Mountain Gems and Beads.

Other ideas for the Mineral World might be crystal, like one from the cluster in the picture above. It should be the same diameter as the stick. Crystals come in many different colors and are believed to amplify energy and increase the connection between what they refer to as the *As Above* (the heavens) and *So Below* (the Earth) This could add a compelling aspect to your sessions.

Attach gems with a little glue and then with leather or sinew. To secure them, begin to wrap the leather at least an inch before the end of the wood and continue the wrap at least another inch on the crystal. Use a thin pliable skin such as deer hide, and then stretch it very tightly. As it dries it shrinks and makes a stronger bond. Soft copper wire, using wire wrapping techniques (available in craft books), can create intricate patterns on the wood and stone and create a beautiful effect. Aside from the favorite rock you found on the beach, you can see fascinating gemstones at rock, gem, or metaphysical stores. A clerk can tell you about the medicine, or energy of the stone. Some jewelry stores carry stones as well.

Jewels have decorated staffs and scepters for millennia. Below is a fourteenth-century scepter carved from malachite with gold and ruby embellishments.

Cabochons are great glued on the ends at a ninety-degree or forty-five-degree mitered cut. Cabochons are stones that have a flat surface on one side. Turquoise is especially sacred to native peoples and is a representation of the land for many, while red coral as a representation of the sea. You might use a piece of turquoise on one end and coral on the other. Many tribes utilize seashells in their decorations, and small ones make beautiful ornaments. If you use a stick with a lot of knotholes, tuck large beads or stones into the holes with a touch of glue.

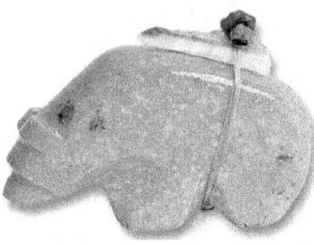

Different animal fetishes or stone animal carvings (totems or allies) can be purchased at gem and mineral stores or found online. The beautiful Zuni turquoise bear fetish is available through the Southwest Indian Foundation.[5] Metaphysical and native stores typically have a wide selection as well. If you see one that represents one of your power animals, you might want to attach it to the top. A friend of mine attached a carved turquoise bear to one end of a stick with copper wire and leather. A stone animal fetish would be a representation of both the Animal and Mineral Worlds.

Leather, of course, is from the Animal World. If you choose a dowel rod, an attractive effect is to wrap the entire stick with thin leather in a spiral fashion. Leather cord or laces can be purchased in many colors as well as regular leather, allowing you to cut your strips. If your stick

---

[5] https://www.southwestindian.com/p/zuni-turquoise-bear-fetish

is an uneven branch, you can wet the leather and stretch it and then let it dry to mold to the surface. I have seen a stick wrapped in rattlesnake skin with the rattles attached at the top with a leather thong.

Leather fringe attached somewhere on the stick is a nice touch but cutting it evenly can be difficult. Stores like Tandy Leather have fringe already cut. Thread the larger glass or stone beads onto the leather strips at intervals and secure with glue. They add a little weight and help create a swingy effect. You might consider small bells too. Native Peoples use bells to draw the Little People, the elves, gnomes, leprechauns, elementals, etc. When you use your talking stick, they should remind you of the value of humor in your life and not to take yourself too seriously.

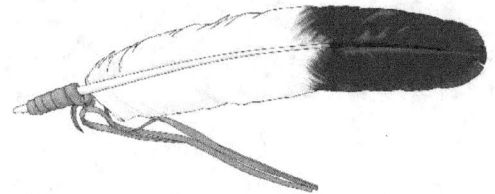

Feathers represent the Winged Ones of the Animal World. Natives feel all birds are a connection to the *As Above* and Great Spirit. Before using any real feathers, consider wrapping the base of the feathers with red thread. Red honors the bird and signifies bringing it back to life. If you do this, consider adding a looped string to the base of the feather and then wrapping with the red thread or string. Do this with several feathers and then attach the bunch to the stick with a leather lace, so they hang free. Cover the thread with leather, or if you are beading your piece, you can bead the base of the feathers as well. The best time of the year to find feathers is in summer when birds are molting, but feathers that look real can be purchased at most craft stores any time of the year if you are unable to find your own.

Under the current language of the **eagle feather law**, individuals of certifiable American Indian ancestry enrolled in a federally recognized tribe are legally authorized to obtain eagle feathers. Unauthorized persons found with an eagle or its parts in their possession can be fined up to $250,000. This law applies to most raptors. The **Migratory Bird Act** makes it illegal to sell the feathers of any migratory bird. If it's a bird that is legally hunted, like waterfowl, it's legal to possess the feathers or give them to someone, but it's illegal to sell them. The laws may sound extreme, but it is vital to protect our wildlife. Introduced game birds, like pheasant, are not covered by the law.

Instead of feathers, some people have used a raccoon or fox's tail. Add a band of rabbit fur or some other type of hair. I have seen horse hair used and buffalo or bear is uniquely masculine. All these animals are sacred to Indigenous Peoples. Skins are available from stores that sell attire for mountain man rendezvous or in American Indian craft stores.

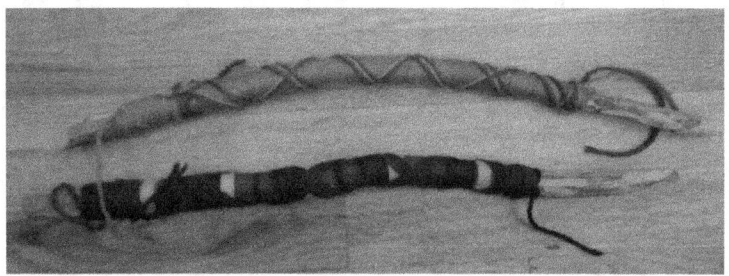

An inexpensive way to create a colorful is to wrap it with yarn. It's fast, and even the youngest of kids can use this technique without waiting for glue to dry, and intricate patterns develop using different colors. Choose wool yarn if you are trying to keep your stick natural.

Adding color by painting is inexpensive also. Two color schemes that have meaning for Native People are the colors of the directions: red, black, white, and yellow. These colors are said to represent the original four races of man. Blue indicates the *As Above*, and the *So Below* is green. The point where the *As Above* and *So Below* meet is usually purple.

The second widely used color scheme is the rainbow: red, orange, yellow, green, blue, purple and indigo. Start at the bottom and paint one-inch wide stripes of each. Of course, you can also paint the stick with any colors that mean something to you.

I also mentioned the Ancestor or Spirit World. Adding something as a remembrance for family members or others who have passed can make a stick very special. My grandfather's Shriner's pin is attached to one of my staffs, and I know a woman in Colorado who is working to get her counseling degree so she can work with veterans with PTSD.

Her talking stick contains military medals of fallen heroes. Any symbol showing your faith or religion would be perfect to represent the Spirit World.

**Use Your Tradition**

The picture on the left above is an African Masai talking stick. Note that the theme of the four directions is featured. The color green replaces the yellow on an American Indian stick.

If you are Irish or Scottish, you might want to give your talking stick a Celtic flair with a Celtic Knot symbol or choose from dozens of others. Above right. The Druids of Celtic heritage and current Wiccans incorporate amazing symbology in their rituals. I have many friends with Celtic-theme staffs. Research your ancestry and create a unique stick.

I did a ceremony with an Irish priest years ago. His talking stick was similar to the royal scepter shown on the next page. I'm not sure of one's age or origins, but I imagine it is solid gold.

**Lastly, and Most Important**

I hope these ideas get your creative juices flowing. Please send me a picture of your completed stick. I would love to add it to my collection.

If you know someone that does native ceremonies, ask them to do a Blessing and Awakening ceremony for your stick, or you can do a simple ceremony yourself using sage or smudge. To make it even more purposeful, separate the individual components of smudge and use them individually indicating their function. Use sage for banishing negative energy and cleansing the item. Sweetgrass' is used for a blessing. Cedar is for balance and stability, and lavender for beauty. Speak your intent as you run your stick through the smoke created by burning each ingredient. After a blessing ceremony, it is customary to present the item to the four directions. After indicating who you are by stating your name, you can say something like, "Sacred ones of the (south). I take the responsibility of being the caretaker of this sacred talking stick. When I use it, I will follow the Talking Stick Rules of Engagement and make sure all speakers are understood. I promise to protect it and use it in a sacred way and always within Sacred Law." Turn clockwise. Face the west, then the north and then the east. Repeat your vow in each direction.

Lastly, NEVER use your talking stick as a weapon.

Walk in beauty, my friend. Awanestica!<br>
In lac'kesh<br>
Mitakuye Oyasin<br>
Namaste'

*Phyllis Two Wolves Dreamer*

# Appendix B
# Guarantee You are Understood Initiative

## *What is the Initiative?*

See the Indicative's description in the section directly following the Table of Contents.

## *Books*

These books available on:
available on www.GuaranteeYouAreUnderstood.com

### Wild Woman Rites of Empowerment Bible - Over 50 Life-Changing Ceremonies

When you purchase this book from the website, we will donate $1 to the selected charity of your choice. See the website for information.

Rites of Passage, or what we call Rites of Empowerment, have helped individuals celebrate the natural evolution of their lives for thousands of years. Today few milestones are celebrated and those that are gloss over and fall short of addressing the emotional issues that mystify and create havoc in our worlds. Indigenous peoples have always observed the natural cycles of change and rites of passage promote the mourning that goes with accepting changes and allows for closure to heal the wounds of our inner child. Ceremonies of Empowerment celebrate our growth and maturation as we travel along our paths as individuals. Rituals balance our masculine and feminine energies and help us regain what Native peoples call the Five Hauquas; health, hope, happiness, harmony, and humor in our lives, which are every human's inalienable rights. The book gives instructions on how to facilitate over 50 life-changing ceremonies. Included are numerous poems and stories to make your celebrations personal and extra special. (2004, 2010, 2019) 396 pages

### Tyler's First Talking Stick (Children's Book) and *Parents, Help Your Child Find Their Voice* (two books in one)
When you purchase this book from the website, we will donate $1 to the selected charity of your choice. See the website for information.

Nine-year-old Tyler had a problem; daily he was tormented by two older boys at school. He was sure his 6'4" father never got bullied when he was in the fourth grade. Tyler was too ashamed to tell his dad until he met Ms. Murphy and held the magic stick.

*Tyler's First Talking Stick* is two books in one. Discover how Tyler found the confidence to talk to his father and resolve his situation at school. Turn the book over for *Parents, Help Your Child Find Their Voice*. This half shows adults how to support children and help them feel comfortable discussing issues they might normally hide from parents or authority figures, concerns that may be vital for their safety.

### Erase Your Past – Change the Future
When you purchase this book from the website, we will donate $1 to the selected charity of your choice. See the website for information.

Have you ever wanted to change your past, knowing that if you did your future would be significantly different? Do certain events from your past influence your behavior or haunt you today? Learn techniques known for millennia by indigenous peoples to erase your past and open doors to a future with unlimited potential.

### Guarantee You Are Understood Facilitator's Certification Guidebook (available 2019 – preorder today).
When you purchase this book from the website, we will donate $1 to the selected charity of your choice. See the website for information.

See the Guarantee You Are Understood Initiative's Vision in the section immediately following the Table of Contents.

The Guarantee You Are Understood Initiative's first goal is to provide a 100% Guarantee that individuals are understood and not just heard in a variety of communication situations. The outcome in many circumstances is vastly improved if sessions are organized and facilitated by an experienced, impartial third party who thoroughly understands the 10 Rules of Engagement that govern Talking Stick sessions. When speakers and dedicated listeners are advised on issues of etiquette, the likelihood of success increases even more.

As a counselor or therapist, add Certified Talking Stick Facilitator to your list of valued skills or become an entrepreneur with your own service. You'll find the answers you need for your own success in this easy to understand guide.

**Guarantee You Are Understood Coach's Certification Guidebook (available 2019 – preorder today).**
When you purchase this book from the website, we will donate $1 to the selected charity of your choice. See the website for information.

The Guarantee You Are Understood Initiative's vision is advocacy for today's kids, teens, young adults, or anyone needing the courage to find their voice. And, specifically for survivors of abuse, whether it be emotional, physical, mental, or sexual. The Initiative's goal is three-fold.

- One. To provide a means for individuals to be 100% understood and not just heard during difficult conversations or conflict resolution. Our approach instills confidence and unique advantages to anyone needing to find their voice.

- Two. To help victims and survivors of abuse overcome emotional trauma and regain dignity. Our methods help individuals repair a broken spirit and retake their power.

- Three. Work with individuals to identify negative behavior patterns in their lives, take responsibility, assume authority, and stand accountable for every thought, word, and deed.

*The Guarantee You Are Understood Facilitator's Guidebook* covers skills necessary for conducting Talking Stick sessions, whether it's between two individuals, families, business associates, all the way to corporate mediation (goal one above).

Goals two and three are covered in this Guidebook and are for those interested in helping victims and survivors of abuse in a deeper capacity.

Every aspect of the Imitative promotes respect and boots self-esteem. Our results are balanced individuals who know their self-worth, demand recognition in society and are ready to take on the world.

Our unique methods fall outside the real of techniques currently used in therapy and are not new; they were used in the earlies times to move and focus energy to intensify the healing process.

These methods are not meant to replace techniques currently use but to complement and enhance strategies and may, at times, be the breakthrough approach that gets results.

You don't need several sets of three-letter designations trailing after your name indicating counselor, masters, or doctoral degrees, to understand the process, although we welcome individuals who are dedicated to coaching, therapy, counseling, or mentoring. For those without the three-letter clusters, the alchemical structure of the ancient process supplements and enhances intuitive skills to help anyone assist others in healing themselves.

You can make a difference.

# Appendix C
# About Phyllis Cronbaugh

Phyllis loves speaking, training, coaching, and writing, (throw real estate in there too) equally. She is President of Life Transition Solutions, LLC, which includes the Guarantee You are Understood Initiative.

Phyllis is available for select readings and lectures. To inquire about a possible appearance, please contact her at pcronbaugh@gmail.com.

**Native American and Indigenous Training**

Phyllis Two Wolves Dreamer brings an intuitive understanding as well as years of training in the spiritual essence of indigenous peoples to her books, workshops, and ceremonies. She believes this knowledge is as valuable today as it has been for millennia in helping us live balanced lives filled with health, hope, happiness, harmony, and humor. As a Twisted Hair (Cherokee, Navajo) and Maya Solar Initiate, she braids traditional knowledge and spirituality together with the modern science of quantum physics, creating a truth that has changed lives and helped many people begin living life to the fullest.

Beginning in the late 90's while she lived in Colorado, Arizona, and California, she apprenticed with a well-known Native American shaman for some years and received other training on native traditions from numerous teachers. Her journey on the Path of the Red Road has taken her to Mexico and Guatemala where she worked and studied with indigenous elders. See Appendix B – Guarantee You Are Understood Initiative and Appendix D – Other Books by Phyllis Cronbaugh.

**National Speakers' Association and Writing**

Phyllis began her training career in 1979 and has owned two training and coaching companies for entrepreneurs. As a member of the

National Speaker's Association and the Colorado and GLAC (Greater Los Angeles) Speaker's Associations, she had opportunities to learn from the best, including Zig Ziglar, Jim Rohn, and others. She says, "The inspiration, motivation, and coaching I received while in NSA, CSA and GLAC were amazing. Everywhere I turned, someone had great advice for me. Without Zig and Dan Kennedy, I'm sure I would never have published my first book or have the confidence in myself that I do today. It's time to pay it forward." Phyllis has written nine books and is planning to have the Guarantee You Are Understood Guidebook out by the end of 2018 and Selling with NO Selling Business Strategies out in 2019. Past Training and Speaking Corporate Clients below.

**Real Estate**

Phyllis holds real estate licenses in Kansas and Missouri and plans to retire when she can no longer climb stairs and open lockboxes. She says, "I love real estate, and thirty years' experience brings the expertise you want working for you when you're making one of the most significant decisions of your life. Every transaction is a puzzle, and I love solving puzzles."

Phyllis got her first Kansas license in 1988 and began buying and flipping trashed-out ski condos in Silverthorne, CO with her late husband in 1990. Currently, she works as buyer's and seller's agents and says that her years of being an investor and working with investors has given her invaluable experience that she passes on to clients. Phyllis loves working with individuals and families referred to her by numerous satisfied clients. She is currently an agent for Platinum Realty.

**Family**

Phyllis makes her home in Olathe, KS with two kitties. She has two stepchildren and four grandchildren. Her step-daughter and son-in-law live in Olathe, and her stepson and daughter-in-law live in Gladstone, ND. As of 2019, her grandson is in master's program in mechanical engineering, and her oldest granddaughter will be a senior in college working on a psychology degree. Two younger granddaughters are in middle school.

**Past Training and Speaking Corporate Clients**

ACA Business Academy, Overland Park, KS
Arapahoe Community College – Littleton, CO
AT&T – New York, NY
Blue River Community College – Kansas City, MO
Boeing Aerospace – Wichita, KS
Cessna Aircraft – Wichita, KS
Cincom Systems, Inc. – Cincinnati, OH
Claim-It Systems, Inc. – Silverthorne, CO
Colorado Mountain College – Breckenridge, CO
Community College of Denver – Denver, CO
Grove Park Inn – Ashville, NC
Front Range Community College – Fort Collins, CO
Hallmark Cards – Kansas City, MO
Hesston Tractor – Hesston, KS
Houston Chronical – Houston, TX
Independence Log Homes – Boise, ID
Johnson County Community College – Overland Park, KS
Joy Manufacturing – Colorado Springs, CO
Kansas City Networking Group – Shawnee, KS
Keller Williams Realty – Kansas City area
Lincoln Public Schools – Lincoln, NE
Log Home Living – Hotel Boulderado – Boulder, CO
Maple Woods Community College – Kansas City, MO
Maytag – Newton, IA
Medical Management Software – San Jose, CA
Medical Management Magazine – San Jose, CA
Metropolitan Community College – Kansas City, MO
Move-Up – Waldo, MO
Olathe Chamber of Commerce – Olathe, KS
Payless Cashways – Kansas City, MO
Penn Valley Community College – Kansas City, MO
Pizza Hit – Wichita, KS
RCPAC – St. Louis, MO
Red Rock Community College – Lakewood, CO
Safelite Auto Glass – Wichita, KS
Santa Fe Railroad – Topeka, KS
State of Kansas – Topeka, KS
Summit County Chamber of Commerce – Silverthorne, CO

United Telecom – Fairway, KS
We Mean Business – Shawnee, KS
Western Gear – Jamestown, ND
Wilderness Log Homes – Plymouth, WI

# Appendix D
# Other Books by Phyllis Cronbaugh

## These Books are Available on Amazon.com

## Business

**Selling with NO Selling Business Strategies**

Selling with NO Selling Business Strategies evolves the mindset of today's businesses and gives them an unsurpassed competitive edge. The strategy creates maximum effect using minimum effort and resources. Targeted prospecting, collaborative relationships; and marketing collateral designed to educate and inform while promoting acceptance, confidence, and trust in buyers unites with the use of next-generation customer relations management applications that can automate up to 75% of mundane daily tasks. The result is long-term profitable, practical, and cost-effective model that can be implemented fast and grows exponentially over time. All this and NO Selling. It's easy to see why many of the networking, marketing, and sales strategies that worked in the past fail miserably today and how easy it is to enhance current procedures to conform to the new mindset. Embracing NO Selling strategies eliminates the stress associated with having to make a sale. A salesperson's true strengths emerge, and they remember why they love their business. (available 2020)

## Real Estate

**Strategic Short Sales: Morally Wrong or Financially Prudent?**

Members of the Real Estate Rescue Network are advocates for individuals and families with distressed properties. Through our experience and extensive training, and that of our strategic partners, we support homeowners as they deal with challenges during this unprecedented time in real estate history. Our network's goal is to educate homeowners and help them explore every option available, beginning with home retention so that they can make informed decisions regarding their futures. Having a network of competent professionals dedicated to seeing homeowners' weather the storm with dignity, integrity, independence and without abuse, neglect, and exploitation is where we start. We don't want to start with foreclosure as an option. The Real Estate Rescue Network is your complete resource from A to Z. (2011) 143 pages

## *Shamanic Fiction*

**Saving the Crystal Skull: An Adventure of Mayan 2012 Prophecy**

Mack MacAlister is enticed into the Guatemala jungle and led to a Maya sanctuary, veiled by mysterious forces for over 10,000 years. He discovers his crucial role in ancient prophecy, remembering his vow from a previous lifetime to save a life-size crystal skull. Guided by Ichtaca, an old shaman, Mack strives to regain the intuitive and magical powers essential to his mission. Against all rationality and amidst turmoil Mack finds his soul mate, Tlalli, and confronts the pain of unfulfilled passion over numerous lifetimes. In a world where only thin membranes separate past, present, and future, Mack pits his will against the crazy Mexican magistrate, Rafael Sánchez, to protect the crystal skull from destruction – for it must open the portal between worlds as the Maya Calendar ends on December 21, 2012 – to prevent destruction of humankind and the Earth. (2010) 332 pages www.SavingTheCrystalSkull.com

**Discovering the Magickal Mysterious Character**

In the spring after Sam's eleventh winter, she meets Grandmother Wisdom Keeper, an old Native American Medicine Woman and begins the journey of her life. The old woman has been waiting for Samantha since her birth, for Sam is destined to become the next Wisdom Keeper far in the future. Sam finds this prophecy overwhelming, yet fascinating and irresistible. Her intense desire to learn the ways of Grandmother's people draw her to discover the beauty of the Path of the Red Road. Grandmother guides Sam with the help of the little people and animals of the forest to find her Sacred Dream; the lessons she has chosen to learn in this lifetime, and the legacy she has promised to leave to the next seven generations. The chapters of her teen years set the stage for Grandmother's lessons, and Sam soon embraces the Magickal Mysterious Character she finds within herself. (2010) 227 pages

## Shamanic Non-fiction

**The Talking Stick – Guarantee You Are Understood and Not Just Heard – Korean version (2014)**
This is the same as the original version but in the Korean language.

# Appendix E
# Resources

**Michael Kravets, MTK Consulting**

Michael Kravets is an educator, writing coach, writer, and editor. He is interested in working with people who are passionate about their stories and want to use their stories to help others. Michael can manage a book project from initial idea generation through final publication. Throughout his career he has helped numerous clients find their voices and become more effective writers.

Michael strongly believes that every writer needs a good editor. A good editor stands in for your readers and helps you see your work from their perspective. The partnership forged between author and editor
- helps the author more easily reach his or her readers
- encourages the author to grow beyond his or her comfort zone
- shows the author how to be the best writer he or she can be.

Michael is ready to help you with your book, book-length project, or any other writing project you may have. Please contact him via email: michael@mtkconsulting.com and mention this book when you do. Visit his website: http://mtkconsulting.com/editorialservices/
LinkedIn: https://www.linkedin.com/in/mkravets/

**Point Graphics, Teresa Carnes and Lori Snow**

Point Graphics has been a woman-owned business since 1998 providing a wide range of products and services, including websites. We specialize in logos but we design and print almost anything you may need for your business. Contact us today to get started on your next graphic design or printing project. We provide personal service at affordable prices regardless of the size of your business. Visit their website: http://pointgraphicskc.com.

# Appendix F
# Simple Talking Stick Structure

**Opening a Talking Stick**

It may sound unnecessary in a casual Talking Stick event, but definitive openings and closings create a structured atmosphere that benefits the entire process.

Use the following steps in most Talking Sticks.

- ☐ Opening – The person who requested the Talking Stick, the designated leader, or individual asked to facilitate, will open the process by stating the reason for the session. They should indicate their position and what their duties will be.

- ☐ Purpose and Desired Result – Discuss the purpose, desired result, and the barometer indicator agreed to by the group in advance. If specific issues are undecided, get an agreement before the session starts.

- ☐ Overview – Deliver a quick, general idea of what to expect, how long the session should last, whether there will be breaks, etc.

- ☐ Format of Talking Stick – Wheel or theater (in most cases, participants will already be seated, and this will not be necessary)

- ☐ Style – Circle or popcorn – Discuss the rotation, protocol, and etiquette of passing the stick at this time, including whether it will go around a designated number of times or until all participants are complete.

- ☐ Timer and Recorder (if applicable) – If using a timer or timing device, the rules need an agreement. It is the same for the recorder. It is not recommended to have a participant of the session as the timer or recorder.

☐ Multiple Points and Notetaking (if applicable) – Remind speakers to break multiple points into small groups or state them individually passing the stick in between. If notetaking is allowed, listeners should be reminded only to jot down keywords.

**Rules of Engagement**

Go over the 10 Rules of Engagement

1. Talking Stick sessions ensure individuals opportunities to speak their mind, be heard and guaranteed they're understood. The process is designed to help repair damaged relationships caused by poor or lack of communication. They can help us reconnect where we have become disconnected and isolated, and give us the opportunity for open, honest discussion.

    ☐ Get agreement that this point is understood.

2. The environment of a Talking Stick should always be one of respect. Sessions should promote respect and boost self-esteem and never humiliate, disgrace, or humble another person.

    ☐ Get agreement that this point is understood.

3. All opinions are valid. We all have different belief systems. We were raised differently and come from diverse backgrounds. Even identical twins raised together have different frames of reference and believe their opinions are valid. We have a right to personal perspectives.

    ☐ Get agreement that this point is understood.

4. Never consider a Talking Stick session unless there is a strong desire to resolve an issue for the highest good of all parties.

    ☐ Get agreement that all parties desire to resolve issues for the highest good of the collective.

5. All participants are equal. Outside status carries no weight within a Talking Stick session, and no one's opinion is more important than another's. A leader has the same rank as all participants.

   ☐ Get agreement that this point is understood.

6. A person can only speak when he or she has the talking stick. When someone has the stick, others must refrain from talking, which includes all comments and gestures even when in agreement, and especially when disagreeing with the speaker.

   ☐ Get agreement that this point is understood.

7. Whatever needs to be said can be said without worry of criticism or judgment. Speakers and listeners should remain open-minded, remembering that all participants deserve to be heard and understood. Someone may be a listener now but will be a speaker before the session is over.

   ☐ Get agreement that this point is understood.

8. Participants will never receive discipline as a direct result of something that is said or revealed during a Talking Stick.

   ☐ Get agreement that this point is understood.
   ☐ If agreed that discipline should be enacted at a future time assuming behavior, circumstances, or conditions do not change, get agreement as to what the punishment is to be, who will discuss it during the session, and other pertinent information.

9. Participants must always speak using "I" statements. No one can speak for someone else unless agreed to before the session begins. Speak for yourself and no one else.

   ☐ Get agreement that this point is understood.

What is said within a Talking Stick session is never discussed with anyone outside the original Talking Stick participants.

☐ Get agreement that this point is understood. If discussions with specific individuals or groups are permitted, make sure to record the names and circumstances.

**Talking Stick Dialog**

    ☐ A Positive Space – Do this before the session starts if applicable. If you plan to Establish the Collective (mentioned next), have the talking stick follow the smudge.

    ☐ Establish the Collective – Even if using a popcorn style of rotation, establishing the collective generally uses one pass (circle style), with each person saying who they are.

    ☐ Begin the Dialog – Follow the directions for the format and style chosen. The speaker should remember to ground themselves and speak openly and honestly.

**Wheel format with circle style and leader (or facilitator)** – When the speaker finishes, they pass the stick to their designated listener who is on their left. When the Guarantee is complete, the listener becomes the new speaker, and the person to their left becomes the newly appointed listener, and the process continues clockwise.

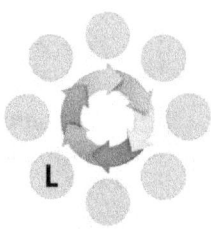

**Wheel format with popcorn style and leader (or facilitator)** – When the speaker finishes, they place the stick in the middle of the wheel, and anyone on the circle may step forward to become the designated listener. When the Guarantee is complete, the listener becomes the new speaker.

**Theater format** – The popcorn rotation is the same as above, and the only significant change is the leader or facilitator formally recognizes the person that accepts the stick. Generally, the speaker remains at the podium or front of the room until the Guarantee is complete and then they take their seat, and formally relinquish the stick to the new speaker.

**Q&A Combo** – The rotation for this session depends on whether a candidate is questioned by a group or a group is questions a candidate. Check the exact rotation that is needed before the session starts.

See Chapter 6 – /Formats and Styles/Q&A Combo.

## Announcing the Completion Status and Ending the Session

Once the barometer indicator is reached, do one of the following:

- ☐ Ending a Session When the Results are Achieved – If ending a segment and preparing to start another, restate the purpose and desired results. Consider passing the stick one last time and ask for reflections.

- ☐ Ending a Session When an Issue is Unresolved – Indicate that the session is being closed with a status of Stalemate or Agreeing to Disagree. If ending with Stalemate, there must be a majority vote for one of two parties or a two-thirds majority for more participants. State the participant's intention for future negotiations. If appropriate, consider passing the stick one last time to ask for reflections.

## Closing a Session

- ☐ Close the event with the same tone as you open. Observe the Completion status in an appropriate manner. Thank everyone for coming and participating. Remember to thank those who did work behind the scenes.

## A Simple Welcoming Session

For a Simple Welcoming session (no Guarantee) consider using only the points below.

- ☐ Opening
- ☐ Purpose and Desired Results
- ☐ Overview
- ☐ Style
- ☐ Rule 1 of the Rules of Engagement: Talking Stick sessions ensure individuals an opportunity to speak their mind, be heard and guarantee there are understood.
- ☐ Rule 5 of the Rules of Engagement: A person can only speak when he or she has the talking stick.
- ☐ Rule 10 of the Rules of Engagement: What is said within a Talking Stick session is never discussed with anyone outside the original Talking Stick participants.
- ☐ Etiquette of Passing a talking stick.
- ☐ Additional Etiquette that may be needed
- ☐ A Positive Space (if applicable)
- ☐ Begin the Dialog
- ☐ End the Session
- ☐ Close

# Appendix G
# Questionnaire for
# Utilizing Strengths of the Participants

(Copy this questionnaire for use in Talking Stick Sessions)

Thanks for agreeing to participate in this Talking Stick session. As a facilitator, I ask that you sit in a specific direction on a wheel or circle to best utilize what you believe are your strengths so that you may benefit the group. You can help me in this process by rating each statement below as to what you feel describes your strengths.

Use 1 for your most reliable quality and 8 for your weakest. Please return this questionnaire to me as soon as possible so that we can prepare for the event.

- [ ] I have an opinion on the Talking Stick subject and feel I can trust myself to be assertive. I have no trouble stating my opinion in an unemotional, neutral, and matter-of-fact manner.

- [ ] I am an adventurous person and don't find myself holding back because of internal, unnamed fears. I am open to trying new things and am looking for the highest good to come from this Talking Stick.

- [ ] I am a take-charge type of person and know how to manifest my dreams. When I put something in motion, I see results soon.

- [ ] I feel I am on a mission to resolve this problem. I know it is something I am supposed to do, and now is the time to do it.

- [ ] I don't feel locked into one solution for this issue. I am open to hearing what everyone has to say and will make up my mind as to the best way to resolve this situation after I understand everyone's opinion.

- [ ] I am an organizer and feel confident that I will be able to help implement whatever resolution the group decides upon promptly.

- [ ] I find myself being the cheerleader in many group functions. I have a knack for holding the group together and seeing the way to resolve tensions when they arise.

I have had experience in dealing with situations such as this before and feel I will be able to bring wisdom to the table along with a desire to see the issue resolved in a timely fashion.

# Appendix H
# Book Club Questions for Discussion

(Answers in Appendix I)

1. How does a Talking Stick session guarantee that someone is understood?

2. Talking Sticks don't allow *he said/she said* accusation arguments. Which rule prevents this?

3. How do you feel a Talking Stick session promotes respect and builds self-esteem?

4. What guarantees that a speaker will not be interrupted during a Talking Stick session?

5. How does a Talking Stick session create excellent listening skills?

6. The author states that Rule 4 of the Rules of Engagement levels the playing field in a Talking Stick session. How does it do that?

7. Rule 7 of the Rules of Engagement states: All opinions are valid. How can all opinions be valid?

8. The nickname of Rule 9 of the Rules of Engagement is the NO Punishment NO Discipline rule. Why is this rule so important?

9. Which of the Rules of Engagement states that parties need to take Talking Stick sessions seriously or not participate?

10. The author told a story called The Office Jerk to a young woman. What was the gist of the story and what was the young woman able to do after hearing it?

11. What's said in Vegas stays in Vegas may be a joke in Las Vegas, but it is not in a Talking Stick session. What makes it important?

12. Describe the meaning of the story of Walking *Around the Wheel*.

13. If someone asks for a Talking Stick session, who chooses where it will take place, who opens the meeting, and who starts the dialog?

14. What kind of uses can you find for a Talking Stick session?

15. What would be the difference between a Fact Finding and Brainstorming Talking Stick?

16. The person opening a Talking Stick session would probably discuss a number of things. Name several.

17. What format and style would you suggest for a board of director's meeting for a large firm discussing changes to stock options?

18. There are several reasons for recording the dialog during a Talking Stick session. Name two.

19. Name a way you might go about *cleansing a space* of negative energy before a session began.

20. What's the difference between a *wheel* and *theater format*?

21. *What is the difference between Agreeing to Disagree* as a status and as an intent?

22. How does a *popcorn style* differ from a *circle* style?

23. There are several reasons for having a consensus on purpose and desired result before a Talking Stick starts. Name two.

24. What would be the best style for a Brainstorming session when the desired result was to decide what features to include in a new product?

25. When would you consider omitting the *Guarantee*? What are the pros and cons?

26. What is a *barometer indicator* in Talking Stick jargon?

27. In the story about Amy's Eating Disorder, why do you think the author felt so strongly about the parents using the event to try to get their daughter into a treatment center?

28. There are several reasons for timing speakers during a session. Name two.

29. How does a leader differ from a facilitator?

30. What is the definition of a *collective* and why do some groups feel strongly about incorporating one in a Talking Stick?

31. What are the first words of the Guarantee?

32. What are some questions that you could have guests answer in a Welcoming session that would get a meeting off to a positive start?

33. What is the difference between *finished* and *complete* in Talking Stick jargon?

34. When would someone be removed from a Talking Stick session and what is required to do so?

35. What should you do if there is a change of purpose or desired results during a session? Is there a specific process?

36. Name two ways that the Guarantee You Are Understood Initiative gives back.

37. How do you become a Certified Facilitator or Coach for the Guarantee You Are Understood Initiative?

38. How does *passing on your right to speak* work? Can you pass on your right to listen?

39. Name some suggestions for notetaking during a session.

40. Describe the protocol for *passing a talking stick*. Why is the eye-lock important?

41. What would be a positive way for a designated listener to answer if the speaker is intentionally or unintentionally exaggerating or doing something to cause drama during a Talking Stick?

42. What can you do to gain confidence before you speak in a session? Name several things.

43. Name several reasons why both the listener and the speaker should *stay in the present* during a session.

44. What might be an answer for a designated listener if they believe the speaker is intentionally trying to change their opinion to another point of view.

45. As the speaker, if you were trying to change someone's point of view, what would be the best way to do it?

46. When may it be a good idea for the designated listener to repeat keywords that the speaker has used and why?

47. What is a good response for the speaker when they realize the designated listener is intentionally or unintentionally miscommunicating dialog?

# Appendix I
# Book Club Answers

1. How does a Talking Stick session guarantee that someone is understood? Answer: The listener must repeat what they understood the speaker to say to the speaker's satisfaction.

2. Talking Sticks don't allow *he said/she said* accusation arguments. Which rule prevents this? Answer: Rule 6: Participants must always speak using "I" statements. No one can speak for someone else.

3. How do you feel a Talking Stick session promotes respect and builds self-esteem? Answer: Rule 2 states: The environment of a Talking Stick should always be one of respect. Sessions should never humiliate, disgrace, or humble another person. The act of looking someone in the eye promotes respect and the fact that everyone's opinion is considered valid builds self-esteem. Actually, every one of the Rules of Engagement is designed to encourage respect and build self-esteem.

4. What guarantees that a speaker will not be interrupted during a Talking Stick session? Answer: Rule 5: A person can only speak when he or she has the talking stick.

5. How does a Talking Stick session create excellent listening skills? Answer: Answer: The designated listener must repeat what the speaker stated to the speaker's satisfaction. Optimally the designated listener will go further and try to *walk in the speaker's shoes* to gain an even better appreciation of why they have that opinion, thus creating an attitude of respect.

6. The author states that Rule 4 of the Rules of Engagement levels the playing field in a Talking Stick session. How does it do that? Answer: Rule 4 states: All participants are equal. Outside status carries no weight within a Talking Stick session, and no one's opinion is more important than another's.

7.  Rule 7 of the Rules of Engagement states: All opinions are valid. How can all opinions be valid? Answer: We all have different belief systems. We were raised differently and come from diverse backgrounds. Even identical twins raised together have different frames of reference and belief systems, and we are all entitled to those beliefs.

8.  The nickname of Rule 9 of the Rules of Engagement is the NO Punishment NO Discipline rule. Why is this rule so important? Answer: Participants can never receive discipline as a direct result of something that is said or revealed during a Talking Stick. Without this rule, there would be no reason for individuals to speak openly and honestly.

9.  Which of the Rules of Engagement states that parties need to take Talking Stick sessions seriously or not participate? Answer: Rule 8 says: Where a resolution is required, all participants should agree to resolve the issue for the highest good of all parties.

10. The author told a story called The Office Jerk to a young woman. What was the gist of the story and what was the young woman able to do after hearing it? Answer: The essence of the story was that a guy, Ted, went into a Talking Stick disliking someone intensely, Harry, but for political reasons felt it was necessary to keep an open mind. During the session, Ted was amazed that his attitude changed towards Harry. He found he had respect for him in a business sense but had not changed his opinion about him as a person. After hearing the story, the young woman was able to set an intention to be open-minded. She went into a session and spoke her mind sincerely and was very surprised that others did not criticize or judge her.

11. What's said in Vegas stays in Vegas may be a joke in Las Vegas, but it is not in a Talking Stick session. What makes it important? Answer: For someone to speak openly and honestly, he or she may need to know the information will go no further than the other party or participants in the session.

12. Describe the meaning of the story of Walking *Around the Wheel*. Answer: Assume that the wheel is life and whatever we see, whether it is a person, place, thing, event, scenario, etc., is placed in the middle. Anyone, even our closest family, and friends will see it differently because we have different frames of reference; we are standing in various places on the wheel. Growing up in the same house does not mean we have the same belief system as others in our household. What everyone sees is valid for their frame of reference or place on the wheel, and everyone is entitled to their opinion.

13. If someone asks for a Talking Stick session, who chooses where it will take place, who opens the meeting, and who starts the dialog? Answer: The person accepting the Talking Stick offer selects the location. The person asking for the meeting does the opening and begins the dialog.

14. What kind of uses can you find for a Talking Stick session? Answer: Welcoming, Brainstorming, Difficult Discussions, Fact Finding, Conflict Resolution, and many more.

15. What would be the difference between a Fact Finding and Brainstorming Talking Stick? Answer: Speed for the most part. Fact Finding is generally more methodical, and brainstorming is spontaneous. The popcorn-style or rotation works well for both, but the circle style may work equally well with Fact Finding.

16. The person opening a Talking Stick session would probably discuss a number of things. Name several. Answer: Purpose, Desired Results, Overview, Type of Talking Stick, Style – Circle or Popcorn, Timer and Recorder, Multiple Points and Notetaking.

17. What format and style would you suggest for a board of director's meeting for a large firm discussing changes to stock options? Answer: Theater format with Popcorn style.

18. There are several reasons for recording the dialog during a Talking Stick session. Name two. Answer: To have a record of participants, so information is not forgotten, and legal reasons.

19. Name a way you might go about *cleansing a space* of negative energy before a session began. Answer: Smudging using a sage stick, crushed sage, sage spray, or sage essential oil in a diffuser.

20. What's the difference between a *wheel* and *theater format*? Answer: In wheel format, participants sit in a wheel shape, or a specified order and the rotation of the dialog is the same every time. Theater format works well for large gatherings such as town meetings, or corporate functions with chairs arranged in rows facing a podium or front table. Popcorn style is generally the rotation of dialog with a theater format.

21. *What is the difference between Agreeing to Disagree* as a status and as an intent? Answer: The status of Agreeing to Disagree is one of three ways to end a Talking Stick. The other two are Stalemate and Success. Agreeing to Disagree signifies that the parties tried for an agreement, but the desired results were not reached for some reason. The reason could be that the results need reevaluation because they are not feasible at this time. The status is not necessarily negative and indicates that the participants may be willing to reconvene at a future date. An intent of agreeing to disagree can be stated before a Talking Stick begins on occasion to relieve any pressure from participants that the session has a hidden agenda or duplicitous motive.

22. How does a *popcorn style* differ from a circle style? Answer: In a popcorn style instead of progressing around the wheel in an ordered fashion, any person in the circle may step forward to be the designated listener when the current speaker is complete, they become the next speaker.

23. There are several reasons for having a consensus on purpose and desired results before a Talking Stick starts. Name two.

Answer: To give guidance and help parties focus their thoughts, so that everyone knows the goal, to keep everyone on track, to gauge progress, and to see when the barometer indicator is reached.

24. What would be the best style for a Brainstorming session when the desired result was to decide what features to include in a new product? Answer: Popcorn style.

25. When would you consider omitting the *Guarantee*? What are the pros and cons? Answer: The Guarantee could be omitted on a Welcoming session. Skipping the guarantee makes the process much faster but incorporating can help participants become acquainted with the designated listener protocol and may prove an efficient way to help everyone remember names and personal information. The Guarantee is rarely used in an *establishing the collective* or *reflection* segments. It is never expected in conjunction with opening remarks or voting rounds.

26. What is a *barometer indicator* in Talking Stick jargon? Answer: The point when it is obvious the desired result is reached or are unobtainable. It indicates that it is time to move to the next step, which could be another segment or ending the Talking Stick session.

27. In the story about Amy's Eating Disorder, why do you think the author felt so strongly about the parents using the event to try to get their daughter into a treatment center? Answer: Rule 9 of the Rules of Engagement states: Participants will never receive discipline as a direct result of something that is said or revealed during a Talking Stick. The author knew that Amy felt that going to a treatment center was punishment for her actions, so this could not be part of the desired result of the session. The author felt a more useful result would be for Amy to discover her solution to regain her abstinence.

28. There are several reasons for timing speakers during a session. Name two. Answer: Setting a limit may force a speaker to think through and present a more concise view, it keeps them

from creating a filibuster whether intentional or unintentional, it suggests an appearance of fairness to allow everyone to speak.

29. How does a leader differ from a facilitator? Answer: A leader can be a participating member of a group that is voted or appointed to hold the position. They must be impartial when the session's protocol requires it but may speak their own opinion freely when they hold the stick or are the designated listener. A facilitator is usually a third party who is entirely impartial and agrees to organize and preside over the session. They have no attachment to the result and will at no time state their own opinion. Both positions must be familiar with the Rules of Engagement.

30. What is the definition of a *collective* and why do some groups feel strongly about incorporating one in a Talking Stick? Answer: A collective is a group that has come together with a common goal. The number of individuals is not significant. Many groups believe that this conscious act of creating and setting a *group intention* helps achieve a favorable conclusion for the gathering. That act is not a mere introduction or clerical step.

31. What are the first words of the Guarantee? Answer: "What I understood you to say was..." and then proceed with what was learned.

32. What are some questions that you could have guests answer in a Welcoming session that would get a meeting off to a positive start? Answer: Where are you initially from and where did you go to school? How did you hear about our group or who invited you? What is something that no one knows about you? What's your favorite restaurant in town and what do you order?

33. What is the difference between *finished* and *complete* in Talking Stick jargon? Finished is when they are ready to pass the stick to the designated listener. They are *complete* when the designated listener has repeated what they understood to

the speaker's satisfaction.

34. When would someone be removed from a Talking Stick session and what is required to do so? Answer: If a participant blatantly refuses to abide by the Rules of Engagement or is disrupting the process to the degree that it is apparent the meeting cannot continue; the remainder of the collective may vote to remove the participant. A unanimous vote is necessary for removal.

35. What should you do if there is a change of purpose or desired results during a session? Is there a specific process? Answer: Changing purposes, desired results, or types of Talking Sticks without explicitly closing one and beginning another isn't recommended. It is suggested to close the current one, take a quick break and then state the new purpose and desired result, and open the next session. Before beginning the next session, remind every one of the relevant decisions from the first, so there is no confusion.

36. Name two ways that the Guarantee You Are Understood Initiative gives back. Answer: First way. When you purchase certain books from the website, $1 is donated to the selected charity of the purchaser's choice. A list of specified charities is available on the website, and the selection is made at the time of purchase.

    Second way. The Initiative trains and certifies facilitators and coaches to use techniques known by the ancients to move energy and to focus and use that energy to enhance healing processes.

37. How do you become a Certified Facilitator and Coach for the Guarantee You Are Understood Initiative? Answer: Work through the certification manual and pass the certification exam.

38. How does *passing on your right to speak* work? Can you pass on your right to listen? Answer: Anyone can *pass* when the stick goes around and pick it up again the next time around. If the person passing is expected to be the designated listener

for the current speaker, they must complete the Guarantee before they pass on their right to speak. You cannot *pass on your right to be the designated listener* unless you state it before the speaker begins.

39. Name some suggestions for notetaking during a session. Answer: To jot down keywords to jog the memory, to never use the time to write or think through responses to the speaker's dialog, to have a hand sign to signal the speaker that a few more moments are needed.

40. Describe the protocol for *passing a talking stick*. Why is the eye-lock important? Answer: When passing the talking stick, hold it with both hands close to the ends and present it to the other person. Wait for them to grasp the stick using both hands toward the middle. Make eye contact and hold it for a second, nod slightly and release the stick it to them. Many indigenous people believe the eyes are the window to the soul. When looking into someone's eyes, the gift of respect is given to the other person.

41. What would be a positive way for a designated listener to answer if the speaker is intentionally or unintentionally exaggerating or doing something to cause drama during a Talking Stick? Answer: "There are two sides to every story. I don't remember it happening quite that way. I'd like you to hear my view. May I share it with you when I am the speaker?"

42. What can you do to gain confidence before you speak in a session? Name several things. Answer: First, take several breaths and relax. Second, be prepared. Try to have planned what you will say. Research your topic is applicable and take notes into the session if it is allowed.

43. Name several reasons why both the listener and the speaker should *stay in the present* during a session. Answer: If a listener's mind wanders to either the past or future, their current view is distorted. Sound may be heard off in the distance or as white-noise. The words of the speaker are not

accurately perceived. To correctly hear and understand the listener needs to stay in the present.

44. What might be an answer for a designated listener if they believe the speaker is intentionally trying to change their opinion to another point of view. Answer: "I understood your opinion is ... That is not my opinion, but I believe that everyone has the right to their own. When I am the speaker, I will be glad to share my view, and I hope you will respect it."

45. As the speaker, if you were trying to change someone's point of view, what would be the best way to do it? Answer: The most effective course of action to get someone to change their opinion is for the speaker to state the argument with confidence along with well-researched reasons why they feel strongly about it.

46. When may it be a good idea for the designated listener to repeat keywords that the speaker has used and why? Answer: The designated listener can show they were actively listening by repeating the speaker's keywords. It can show empathy and indicate they understood what they heard. Using a word, the listener feels equal, but the speaker feels is misconstrued could derail the session.

47. What is a reasonable response for the speaker when they realize the designated listener is intentionally or unintentionally miscommunicating dialog? Answer: "I believe you understood me on ..., ..., and ..., but I guess I didn't make myself clear on ..."

www.ingramcontent.com/pod-product-compliance
Lightning Source LLC
Chambersburg PA
CBHW071533220526
45469CB00003B/767